FAST
BY THE ROAD

THE MACMILLAN COMPANY
NEW YORK · BOSTON · CHICAGO · DALLAS
ATLANTA · SAN FRANCISCO

MACMILLAN AND CO., Limited
LONDON · BOMBAY · CALCUTTA · MADRAS
MELBOURNE

THE MACMILLAN COMPANY
OF CANADA, Limited
TORONTO

FAST
BY THE ROAD

By

JOHN MOODY

New York

THE MACMILLAN COMPANY

1942

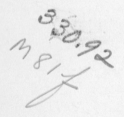

TO MY WIFE

*Without whose sympathetic interest
and constant encouragement
this book would never have been
brought to completion.*

PREFACE

WHEN JOHN MOODY permitted me to see the first chapters of *The Long Road Home*, I remember being astonished that so busy a man could have done the wide reading indicated in that volume. Evidently he had not confined himself to the usual solace of the tired business or professional man—detective stories—or to current periodicals or fiction or biography or popularized history, or even to the standard works of English literature. He had delved into philosophy, theology and even mysticism. Naturally, a hard-bitten editor was inclined to suspect pose or pretense. But as I continued to read, I came to realize that the author had, as Francis Bacon recommends, not "tasted and swallowed" but "chewed and digested" these substantial works.

Now that I have come to know him more intimately, we sometimes play a little impromptu game of Question and Answer. I ask, "Have you read such and such?", deliberately selecting something rather recondite. Seldom is he stumped. I discovered, for example, that he had read Dom Augustine Baker's *Sancta Sophia* three times!

I hasten to say that John Moody's erudition does not, so to say, rise up and slap you in the face or stick a thumb in your eye. It hides itself and can be detected only by those who read between the lines. The reader will sense rather than see in a line or paragraph, evidence of acquaintance with the best ancient or modern thought. John Moody can "take" learning or "leave it alone." Generally, he leaves it alone. He prefers anecdote, humor, pleasantry.

For this reason *The Long Road Home* and this, its sequel, *Fast By the Road*, are, I think, unique. Other attempts have been made to present Catholic doctrine and Catholic life in a popular way, with abundance of illustrative explanation. But I think I have never previously come across a volume that describes so entertainingly what we Catholics believe and think and do. There used to be a little book called *French Without Tears*. Mr. Moody has done better than that. He has given us theology with chuckles. Those, therefore, who balk at a didactic book need not shy away from anything written by this most unusual "Wall Street man." There is plenty of fun in this volume as in its predecessor. Not riotous fun, of course, not wise-cracks or slapstick, not jokes for jokes' sake, but quiet merriment woven like the woof into the warp of a substantial piece of spiritual autobiography.

The method is that of Abraham Lincoln who, though he doubtless told many a story just for the fun that was in it, usually said, "Gentlemen, that reminds me," when he wanted to elucidate a point in politics, or to inculcate a lesson in simple humanity. So with John Moody. Just at the moment when you might fear that he is about to slay you or bore you (to bore is to slay) with a theological argument, he sidles away into an anecdote with an ingratiating "That reminds me." When the anecdote is finished you have both the amusement and the lesson.

By this time someone may suspect that I am inclined to think well of this unusual book. But see for yourself.

JAMES M. GILLIS, C.S.P.

TABLE OF CONTENTS

FOREWORD

MORE THAN TEN YEARS have gone by since I embraced the Catholic Faith and was received into the Church. And it is just about fourteen years since I first began to turn my thoughts in that direction.

In the closing chapters of *The Long Road Home,* a brief autobiography written nearly a decade ago, I told of some of my experiences in approaching the Church and my reasons for becoming a Catholic. I had not expected to add anything to that confession of faith; but as the years have since rolled on I have found that there are many more confessions to be made; many new experiences have come my way which might reasonably be brought to light. Moreover, lengthening perspective of course enables me to envision my pilgrimage in a far more intelligible fashion than would have been possible at the time of my conversion.

And I suppose I cherish the impulse (as many another convert does) to let the critics and doubters know that my life in the Church has not resulted in disappointment or disillusion. After all these years I find persons occasionally asking me if I am still a Catholic, and if so, have I found all I hoped for in my new home. Has the realisation been equal to, or better than the promise? And then of course, there are the incorrigible sceptics; those who are sure, regardless of what you tell them, that you have long since decided that it was all a mistake but are ashamed to admit it—it now being far too late to do anything about it.

To all inquiries about the Catholic Faith and what it has meant to me, I answer the best I know how; but like many another I am often too inarticulate to answer with the lucidity the subject most surely demands—finding it far better to write things down; to state my case on paper. In any event, mere verbal expositions of the Faith or of one's reasons for embracing it, are usually quite chaotic, or at least incomplete. That is why they so often go in one ear and out the other, and are forgotten by the inquirer in no time at all.

Perhaps these are some of the reasons why, after over ten years of Catholic life, I am venturing to inflict another book upon the public. We converts usually know all too little when we first come into the Church; and it was so with me. I knew considerable about the Church's teachings; her logic drew me, her proofs convinced me. But did I then know enough to keep me a believing and practicing Catholic for all the remaining days of my life? Perhaps not; perhaps only time could teach me enough for that.

It is certainly true that both men and women approach the Catholic religion from many different angles. Indeed, it is often said that there is a different approach to the Church for every convert. There is for instance, the so-called "intellectual" approach. It is claimed by many that this is the ideal approach; and in one sense this is undoubtedly true. But we often hear of persons who "accept" Catholic truth intellectually, and yet we notice that they continue to remain outside the Church. They seem to content themselves with merely agreeing that the Catholic Faith is true and irrefutable. But they do not come in. One wonders why. Perhaps it is because they have not made a sufficient study of the respective merits of pride and humility!

That, at least, was my own position for a long time before I made any positive move to enter the Church. I was quite convinced of the soundness of the Catholic version of Christianity, but—there I stood.

What was it, exactly, that finally brought me in? Was it intellectual knowledge of Catholic philosophy, research and study of Catholic history, full understanding of the synthesis of Catholic dogma? Not at all. All these things enlightened and guided me, but they did not bring me in. What finally brought me in was A LIFE. Not until the stupendous significance of Jesus Christ as the Incarnate God had risen before me; not indeed until I began fully to understand that Christ lives in His Church today as truly, as objectively, as He lived in Palestine nineteen hundred years ago, did the Catholic Church have much more than an incidental or "intellectual" interest for me. But when, with the help of divine grace, I clearly grasped this mighty truth, all doubt was left behind. The full reality of the Living Christ in His Church had opened to my vision.

. . .

Throughout the chapters of this book an attempt has been made to explain in simple language or by illustration, certain teachings and viewpoints to be found within the Church which are often misunderstood or misinterpreted by non-Catholics. All this is merely incidental to the general purpose, which is primarily to tell of some of the experiences of one convert during his first decade as a Catholic. And let me say in relation to this personal aspect, that as I have labored over this attempt to show how the blessed vision of Truth has enriched my Catholic years, it has not been without misgivings that I have found it necessary to make my story an all too egocentric one, mainly centered on my own personal thoughts and doings. And yet how else could I write of what I have dared to call my pilgrimage of grace?

After all, if life is a pilgrimage, it is a personal pilgrimage; a personal matter for every soul. And since it is with sympathetic interest that I read the confessions of other pilgrims, I am encouraged to hope that the following chapters, unimportant and trivial though they be, may prove of some interest or be of some help to others who have found or have yet to find the goal. We do not stand still after we have found Truth; we go on to new experiences, broadening visions, longer perspectives. The Catholic Faith is never grasped in its fullness at the outset; with every convert—as indeed I suppose with *every* Catholic—it is a growth, a development, an unfolding.

J. M.

Camp Solitude,
Merriewold, New York,
October, 1941.

CHRISTIANITY came into the world firstly in order to assert with violence that a man had not only to look inwards, but to look outwards, to behold with astonishment and enthusiasm a Divine Company and a Divine Captain. The only fun of being a Christian was that a man was not left alone with the Inner Light, but definitely recognized an outer light, fair as the sun, clear as the moon, terrible as an army with banners.

—G. K. Chesterton, in *Orthodoxy*

FAST
BY THE ROAD

Chapter One

GOOD-BY TO ALL THAT

1.

SOME YEARS AGO a friend who had just been reading *The Long Road Home*, said to me, "I'm not much impressed by your conversion to the Catholic Church, but I am impressed by your romanticism. You dramatize various incidents in a way which makes your story read much like romantic fiction. Isn't it mostly fiction? I don't mean the incidents you recount; they may all be true enough. I mean the interpretations of them which you weave into your story. Honestly now, aren't these interpretations mostly after-thoughts?"

No doubt a lot of them were after-thoughts; after appraisals of events which led up to my conversion. But what of that? Why should I not try to interpret the meaning of my own experiences?

And so with this attempt to write of some further experiences, which have come my way during these later Catholic years. Some things in the following pages may indeed be tinged with or illuminated by after-thoughts. But should there seem to be any romanticism in what I am now about to write, I can assure the reader that it will be merely the romanticism of truth. There is often a more romantic ring to truth than to fiction or fancy.

More than once have I been told that I became a Catholic

because I am too romantic—and also because I am too un-romantic. And then there are those who say I became a Catholic because I am too credulous; offset, however, by those who say I am too sceptical. And finally, there are those who say I am too serious and lack a sense of humor. Perhaps. But then I do know a lot of people who accuse me of being too frivolous about serious things and too intrigued by humor. Some have even said that I must have become a Catholic merely "for the fun of the thing."

However, some of the critics are more sympathetic. There are always to be found, on the occasion of a conversion to the Catholic Faith, certain kind Protestant or pagan friends who urge you to go in and eagerly tender their good offices to help you get in. "I don't need it but perhaps you do," is their usual refrain. One of these kind friends, on hearing of my intention to become a Catholic, immediately offered to facilitate for me (through one of his influential Catholic acquaintances) an introduction to the late Cardinal Archbishop Hayes. "That will get you in at the top," said he; "it will make your reception into the Church an outstanding event." That is to say, I would be able to get a lot of publicity—the one thing I wished to avoid.

Of course I had no desire to "get in at the top," nor make my act "an outstanding event." I wanted it to take place as quietly and modestly as possible. And so I chose for the place of my reception a little Dominican convent chapel up in the hills of Sullivan County, New York, not far from my summer home. But to certain sceptics even that looked like trying to get in at the top, for it did happen that I had the privilege of meeting the Cardinal right there only a few weeks before my reception into the Church took place.

There was no premeditated planning about that, however.

As a matter of fact, up to that time I had not known any priests, not to mention cardinals, archbishops or bishops. There had been but two or three instances in my life where I had even spoken to a bishop or priest. Some ten or fifteen years before, it had happened that I had given a little lecture on finance to some of the students of St. Louis University, and there I did meet a priest (whose name I have long forgotten) and was introduced to and spoke for a few moments with a bishop (whom I have since discovered was Archbishop Glennon). But there was no talk on religion that night; it was all Wall Street stuff. I recollect saying to the boys that the main job of the Wall Street broker was to "temper the wind to the shorn lamb." That was as close as we got to religion on that occasion.

The only other instance when I talked with a priest prior to meeting the one who received me into the Church, was back in the year 1926 in Le Touquet, France, where I was staying a short time that summer. A shabby little padre stopped me on the street and asked me for a few francs to help his poor. I spoke briefly with him in my pidgin French, gave him twenty francs, and was immediately reprimanded by an American then living in France, who happened to be with me at the moment. "I hope I am broadminded," he said, "but I urge you never to give money to these French priests; they are always looking for it. Besides, it's a mistake to help the Catholic Church even in that small way." Broadminded! My immediate impulse was to hurry after the departing padre and give him a few more francs.

But while I had never talked religion with priests and knew but few lay Catholics—none seeming able or willing to tell me very much about the Catholic Church—I had nevertheless often discussed Catholicism with numerous Protestant friends. Not that this was of much help to me, for it generally turned out that they knew less about the subject than I did. But, as an old friend of Protestant affiliations one day said, "You seem to enjoy annoying us Protestants by making it a point to ridicule us on every possible occasion."

Only too true; I fear I was often very uncharitable. And perhaps that was on my conscience later on, for I recall experiencing a considerable feeling of chagrin when the first thing impressed upon me by my spiritual director after being received into the Catholic fold, was the duty of being tolerant and charitable towards those of other beliefs. As a good Catholic one should avoid throwing stones, should not forget the amenities—a bit of sound instruction perhaps often needed by the militant convert who has just kicked the ladder from under him.

That, I think, was my first Catholic lesson in correct conduct. To aggressively defend your Faith was your duty, but to deliberately ridicule people of other beliefs was distinctly uncharitable. "You must remember," I was told, "that many of these sincere people who do not see eye to eye with you, are nevertheless in good faith."

After that cold douche I did try to reform. While I may have occasionally fallen from grace, I believe I can say that, as a rule at least, it was from then on good-by to all that.

2.

I now found myself using the phrase, "Good-by to all that," in connection with many things that I had left behind. It was, of course, a definite good-by to my old life of uncertainty and unsettlement; a good-by to my former moods of doubt and despair; as well as a most consoling good-by to my long held notion that "Modernists," in the fields of religion and philosophy, in springing their perennial novelties on the public, were disclosing new and important things about life.

Moreover, it was a most gratifying good-by to the fancy, so ingrained with many non-Catholics, that to embrace the Catholic Faith one must assume a sanctimonious air and suppress one's sense of humor. For I promptly found that the Catholic life is as redolent of humor as it is of joy. I had always felt that I was quick to see the funny side of things, but after settling down in the Catholic Church I soon began to envisage far more clearly than ever before, the difference between real jokes and flat jokes; and I now began clearly to see that all my past divagations in the field of modern philosophy had been just one long flat joke.

Only those who have spent years in trying to follow the lucubrations of modern thought, can understand the relief one undergoes when one realizes that it is not at all important to keep in touch with the latest views of a Bertrand Russell, a John Dewey, a Harry Elmer Barnes, or any of the smaller stars of this constellation; that it is not worthwhile paying any attention when some pseudo-scientist gets into the newspapers with the hoary old claim that he is on the track of a chemical or other materialistic formula for discovering the origin of life; or when, in the field of so-called religious humanism, one more oracle claims to prove that the records show that traditional Christianity has not any tangible evidence for its truth.

Not only these but most of my good-bys were tinged

with joy. If there were any exceptions it was only in those few cases where old friends were grieved or shocked. But such incidents were few. The only one that now remains in my memory was in connection with a serious old friend who, when the news began to leak out, rushed to a mutual acquaintance and in a state of panic, exclaimed:

"There's a libelous story going around that our old friend John Moody has joined the Romish Church. It's a lie; I don't believe it. Someone is trying to ruin him. Let's go and tell him about it." And when he found it was true he went to bed with a fever. Poor old chap; I'm afraid he never forgave me.

But after all, that was a very minor incident. When the news finally got into the daily papers a flood of mail trickled in from strangers from all across the country. The Kukluxers, the Rutherfordites, the Pope baiters and the champions of all sorts of strange religions were promptly on the job. In one week I received more K-K-K literature than I had ever seen in my life before; and I had seen much. But that sort of anti-Catholic propaganda had never impressed me, even in my most pagan days. It never rang true.

More interesting were some of the personal letters from strangers. One of the most extraordinary was from a pious prophet living in the Bronx, New York City. He wrote at great length, assuring me that I had by no means found the true Church of Christ. *He* had found it. Not only had he found it but he had *founded* it with twelve apostles of his own selection. And he went on to explain that as one of his twelve had turned out to be a Judas Iscariot, there was now a vacancy in his apostolic college. He invited me, if I would

but conform to his gospel, to become his St. Matthias, and
fill the vacancy.

There were letters from the more orthodox also. One
grand old fundamentalist who then occupied the pulpit of
a large city church of the Baptist persuasion, where for
years he had been ringing the changes from his pulpit on
hell-fire and brimstone, sent me a long, carefully worded
letter, pointing out the frightful Catholic "heresies" I had
apparently overlooked, and urging me to reconsider before it was too late. If I would but emulate the example of
the prodigal son, he promised me a station of distinction in
his own communion. And he closed by warning me of the
wrath to come if I ignored his kindly offer.

Then there was a pious old revivalist of the evangelical
type who, reading in a newspaper interview that the writings of St. Thomas Aquinas had influenced me, sent this
gem: "I always supposed Thomas Aquinas was only one
of them ignorant old monks. So he wrote a book you say?
What did he call it and where can I get a copy?"

I suggested that he first read Dr. Fulton Sheen's masterly
interpretation of the philosophy of St. Thomas—*God and
Intelligence* [1]—which had been my own first introduction
to the subject. But he would have none of that; he wanted
"no Catholic distortions!" And so I referred him to the
Dominican translation of the *Summa Contra Gentiles* in
six volumes! That must have been discouraging, for he
dropped the matter then and there.

The foregoing are mere samples of many communica-
tions received from strangers. I could add dozens of similar

[1] *God and Intelligence in Modern Philosophy*, by Fulton J. Sheen,
M.A., Ph.D., Longmans, Green & Co., New York, 1925.

types. There seemed to be one characteristic about nearly all these letters from this host of unknown critics. Few seemed to sense the fact that I might have become a Catholic for the simple reason that I had found Catholicism to be the true Christianity. That was the simple answer; all too simple, perhaps, for this anvil chorus.

But after all, the interest shown by many strangers was not outstandingly critical; some were very friendly and sympathetic. I recollect one charming letter from a prominent Anglican clergyman, who most enthusiastically congratulated me for cutting myself loose from the confusions and contradictions in which, he said, he was himself enmeshed. And I rejoice to say that there were few estrangements or severing of real friendships. Indeed, it seems to me as I look back now, that while some friends failed to understand and suggested absurd reasons for my conversion, there was really a sincere "God speed you," from the vast majority.

And so it has been throughout all the years of my Catholic life. Kindliness, tolerance and sympathy from those not of the Faith, have heavily outweighed the sporadic criticisms of the intolerant few. I only hope my attitude towards them has been equally kind. Certainly I have tried to keep it so.

3.

Perhaps this is the place where I might properly explain, at some length, one of my most significant good-bys. I wish to do so with tolerance and sympathy towards certain sincere Christians whose view on one religious phase is quite the reverse of my own.

When a convert to Catholicism comes out of the Prot-

estant Episcopal Church it is often assumed by those who
do not know the facts, that he must have been already
nine-tenths Catholic, and had therefore made but a minor
change. This assumption arises from the fact that one group
in the Protestant Episcopal Church, and a similar group in
the Church of England, call themselves "Anglo-Catholics."

Now I had never called myself an "Anglo-Catholic."
Long before that term came into wide use in this country,
I had dropped out of the High Church section of the Protestant Episcopal communion, had wandered in and out of
the Low and Broad sections, and finally landed in the vortex
of Modernism. And although later on I lost all confidence
and interest in this modernistic confusion, I never went
back to the High Church point of view.

Nevertheless I always retained a certain affection for
this High Church group—who nowadays call themselves
"Anglo-Catholics." They, at least, seemed to have a definite faith, and although by no means uniformly in agreement, one could usually tell, with fair accuracy, what they
believed—at least in essentials. This had seemed far from
true with the Broad and Modernist sections, where doctrinal beliefs were being frequently revised, revamped, re-
stated or removed.

I still have a warm spot in my heart for the "Anglo-
Catholics." The insight I often get of the sincere life of
faith many of them lead, commands my deep respect. Yet
they are a puzzle to every informed and observing Catholic.
As a priest remarked to me one day when we were discussing them: "It surely must be that these Anglo-Catholics
are strongly endowed with the virtue of fortitude—especially the sincerely believing laity. Living within a
Church split into several schools of thought, with no real

head to lead or guide them; obliged to recognize and live under bishops who in many instances contradict or even ridicule their cherished beliefs, it is truly amazing that they can cling to their notion that the Protestant Episcopal Church is a part of the Visible Church on earth which Christ founded."

Most certainly they are endowed with fortitude; a degree of fortitude I never could muster. Many times have I been asked why I did not go over to the "Anglo-Catholics" instead of going to all the trouble of becoming a Roman Catholic. It would have been so simple. All I would have had to do would be to switch my attendance from a Broad or Low church to a High—and no questions asked. Just step across the street, so to speak.

But fortunately for me I had already been there and knew all about it. Although as an "Anglo-Catholic" I might feel free to hold all the essential beliefs of the Catholic Faith (aside from the Supremacy of the Pope), the way I would have to hold them would be quite foreign to the way the real Catholic holds them. For the only way I could possibly hold them would be the Protestant way.

If I claimed to accept these Catholic doctrines on the authority of the Church—as "Anglo-Catholics" say they do—just what would I mean by that? I would mean, of course, a species of "authority" gleaned by myself from the teachings of the Christian Church of antiquity, picking and choosing, on my own or some other person's judgment, what I liked, or what some other person told me to like; but feeling free to reject what I did not like. That is precisely what Martin Luther did; what John Calvin did; that is the time-worn Protestant method of private judgment.

But I wanted to be a *Catholic*, not a Protestant. And the

Catholic conception of the authority of the Church is quite different from this "Anglo-Catholic" (Protestant) idea. The Catholic's authority is that of a still living Church which speaks and commands here and now. The Catholic Church did not cease to speak with divine authority after the first few centuries. If she then spoke with the authority of Christ, she speaks with that authority now.

And so it is that to be a Catholic you must become a member of this body which is held together not merely by the personal opinions of her members, but by something far stronger than that. You have a living, divine authority acting upon you, disciplining and directing you. This authority is real to you and effective, because you know with certainty (a certainty based not on mere subjective fancy but on objective facts) that it is the living voice of Christ Himself. You merge yourself in unity and solidarity with this teaching Church of divine creation, which is uniform and universal in her teachings of faith and morals, and speaks on these matters with the infallible authority delegated by Christ to His Vicar, the Pope.

If a convert, you have of course—coöperating with divine grace—reached your decision to become a Catholic through your own free will and private judgment. But once a Catholic, you submit yourself to the authority of the Church. And you obey your Catholic bishops without question, for you know that they never contradict one another in the field of faith and morals, but that they invariably speak on these matters with the authority of Christ as voiced by the Holy See. "It hath seemed good to the Holy Ghost and to Us," are the words of that authoritative voice.

How different this is from the Protestant method of the "Anglo-Catholic." The latter does claim that his Protestant

Episcopal bishops possess apostolic orders and therefore speak with apostolic authority; and yet at the same time he insists that he, as a lay "Anglo-Catholic," has the right, and that it is often his duty, to ignore or defy these bishops when they dispute his cherished Catholic beliefs. What fortitude it must call forth to live in peace with that contradiction!

But happily for me, I was easily able to say good-by to all that, and choose Catholic certitude, with its blessed condition of unity and peace.

4.

Finally, I might say a few words about one more important good-by. Despite the fact that I had been for many years a member in good standing of the Protestant Episcopal Church and had now bid a last good-by to that, this does not imply that I had no other religious or philosophical ideas to shake off. A really more significant thing than my turning away from Protestantism, was my abandonment of the materialistic outlook which, for a great many years, undoubtedly had a far greater influence on my life than any religious convictions I may have had, or fancied that I had.

Those of us who were growing into manhood during the last two decades of the nineteenth century can easily recall to mind what was then being assiduously taught to the youth of the day in most of our secular halls of learning. It was the heyday for popular dissemination of the Darwinian hypotheses. Charles Darwin, with Thomas H. Huxley, John Tyndall, William Kingdon Clifford and Herbert Spencer were the great recognized authorities teaching the simian ancestry of mankind. We were being taught that man, as a rational animal, was, in both body and soul, merely an outcome of evolutionary processes, having developed through the ages by means of "natural selection" from lower orders of living things; these lower orders themselves having evolved, throughout aeons of time, from inanimate matter.

There was no explanation of the *origin* of inanimate matter; that problem was laid aside as one of the mysteries which would sooner or later be solved through scientific advance. It was taught that it was far more significant to know the processes of evolution by which man had risen from the slime to his present high estate, than to know how life originally came to be.

Thus were sown the seeds of a scientific justification of the modern theory of inevitable human progress through mere material change; the theory that mankind, through a purely materialistic process, was steadily climbing upwards spiritually and intellectually as well as physically. Our own age of resplendent scientific advance was held to be proof of the truth of all this. Civilization was now speeding towards perfection; the real Utopia was not far away. If the nineteenth was the greatest of centuries for having discovered the rise of man from a simian start, the twentieth century would, through further scientific advance, ratify the truth of this philosophy.

In the light of such teaching, we youngsters of the late 1880's and early 1890's saw little facing our lives except a steadily rising tide of material progress and prosperity. The catch phrases of those days were: The survival of the fittest, the upward and onward march of civilization; and to many, the devil take the hindermost. We were all very sure that the millennium was just ahead of us; it would be ushered in with flying colors with the further great scientific advance of the twentieth century.

Religion? That was our religion, even though many of us gave lip-service to some more spiritual conception of life. We usually classed the most successful people as the truly righteous ones; those who devoted their lives to the attainment of financial affluence or social standing; those industrious ones who strove to "make two blades of grass grow where one grew before"—which, alas, only meant for most of us, putting two dollars in our pockets where there was but one before. For even while we willingly voiced the Scriptural text that the love of money is the root of all evil, devotion to the almighty dollar was the touchstone of all our striving.

With this early teaching deeply implanted in us, we were naturally ripe, as we merged into maturity, for all the later developments of materialistic philosophy; the pragmatism of William James, the agnosticism of George Santayana and of Bertrand Russell; and, of course, for most of the absurdities of Freudianism.

That sort of mental training made it quite logical for us to become devotees of Hegelian idealism—out of which has finally been brought to the ascendent in our day the totalitarian State, with the relegation of the masses to the rôle of slaves of the State; and, beginning in Russia, the launching on a large scale of the Communistic programs of Karl Marx and Friedrich Engels, involving the ultimate annihilation of religion and the enthronement of atheism.

Today we are far into the twentieth century, which was to bring to fruition this gospel of inevitable human progress through material change—as so widely taught in my youth.

And what do we see before our eyes, now that the predicted Utopia is so long overdue?

We see a world armed to the teeth; wars going on all over the globe; class arrayed against class, nation against nation, with hate the dominating motive of men in slaughtering their fellows. We see all but worldwide greed, envy and hate; the sanctity of human life all but forgotten; the moral law gone with the wind. Where now is the upward and onward march of civilization? What does one now call the survival of the fittest? In short, what has this widely proclaimed, farreaching scientific advance done to mankind?

I would not wish for a moment to give the impression that I followed, with full and conscious acceptance, this materialistic philosophy, so widely taught in my youth; nor that the seeds then sown ever flowered in full with me. In fact, whatever interest I had was always tempered with doubt. But to quite a substantial degree those early teachings of Huxley and Spencer, and the later developments of them by James, Santayana, Dewey and Russell, profoundly influenced, for many years, my own outlook on things both human and divine. I surely did drift with that current right down to the time of my awakening to the truths of Catholic teaching.

I rejoice, however, that it did not require the world cataclysm, which we see before our eyes today, to induce me to repudiate every vestige of this false outlook on life. I am not one of those who have waited for the proofs that the devastating teachings sown in the days of my youth regarding the origin, nature and destiny of man, would culminate in an age of bestiality and barbarism such as has not been known in all history since the days of the Caesars at the dawn of Christianity. Nor am I caught in that muddle of mental confusion, so characteristic today of many well-wishers of better things, who *still* seem to be living on the husks of that false philosophy of inevitable human progress through scientific advance.

Fortunate indeed I was to have been able, more than a decade ago, to bid a complete good-by to all that, when through the grace of God, I discovered and embraced the Catholic Faith—and in so doing rediscovered the old true doctrine, not of the rise, but of the Fall of Man.

CHAPTER TWO

THE PEARL OF GREAT PRICE

1.

"I CANNOT UNDERSTAND how a man of your intelligence and lifelong experience as a man of the world could do such a thing as to embrace the Catholic Faith. If you were young and emotional and sentimental it would not be so puzzling to me. But you are old, hard-boiled and —I have always thought—very hard-headed. How can a hard-headed citizen deliberately entangle himself with an institution like the Catholic Church? To me it's a mystery; and, if such a thing could be, I would call it a miracle."

So remarked a hard-boiled and hard-headed friend of mine some years after I had become a Catholic. It was a mystery to him and—maybe—a miracle. The remark immediately reminded me of another conversation of my early Catholic days. I was sitting in the corner of the smoking section of a Pullman, deeply buried in a book, when a stranger sitting opposite and smoking a cheap cigar, watched me a while and then said:

"You seem to have an absorbing yarn there, brother. What is it? Detective stuff? Sex stuff?"

"Neither," I replied. "It's called *God and the Supernatural*. About as far away as you could get from detective stuff or sex stuff, I imagine."

17

"Oh, *heavy* stuff. I never go in for that. But I sometimes do get a kick out of a good mystery story."

"Well," said I, "this is really a mystery story of the first water. It's all about the mysteries of God and of the super-natural order."

"What 'order' is that? You don't mean Masons?"

"Far from it. I mean the supernatural mysteries of the Christian religion. This book explains and gives you the answer to all these mysteries."

"Religious stuff? I don't go in for that either. That's just wish-fancy, brother; faith stuff; you just imagine things. Take it from me, there's nothin' in it. It's like believing in miracles; they just don't happen, you know. Here, have a cigar." It was a deadly five-center, but out of politeness I lighted it.

"Strikes me," I said, "that you are something of a miracle yourself. How do you come to breathe, think, talk and so on? How comes it that you are a living person and able to function as you do on this earth for a lot of years? Wouldn't you call that a mystery—or a miracle? What's back of it all, the cause of it all?"

He looked hard at me for a moment, obviously trying to think out an answer. Then, letting his cigar ash fall on his vest, he shrugged his shoulders and said, "I'm damned if I know. That *is* a mystery—if it ain't a miracle. You are right about that, brother."

"Yes, it's a mystery all right. And this book I am reading undertakes to unravel and give the answer to it all."

"Let's see that book." He reached over for it. "Hmm— hmm—this *is* heavy stuff. Too deep for me. Pious stuff; religious stuff. Hmm—hmm. Well, it's a mystery to me how such an intelligent-looking chap as you can plough through a big dry book like that. It would be a headache for me." He closed the book and handed it back.

"There you are," I commented. "You agree that you are yourself a mystery; that life is mystery. You like to read a good mystery story. Why? To see the mystery unraveled; to get the answer. So do I. That's what I am looking for in this book—the answer to a lot of mysteries."

Obviously he was bored; not interested. "Oh yeah," he said, as he tossed his cigar butt away and arose and started for the door; "I wish you luck, brother. I agree; life is a hell of a mystery. Good night!"

Two sample attitudes towards Catholic Christianity. My friend, whom I quoted first, was really interested in religion, but too prejudiced to ever look into Catholicism. The stranger was not at all interested in religion of any kind. "Faith stuff" was just a bore.

And yet I can understand them both; for as I glance back to the time when I knew nothing about Catholicism I realize that my own attitude was in many respects similar. After all, no one can really understand Catholicism from the outside. One must be on the inside to have a full understanding. For some years I tried to understand it from the outside. Perhaps I did learn a little by this method. At least I learned that nearly everything derogatory to the Church as proclaimed by anti-Catholic commentators was distinctly not true. And I also learned at long last that the true way to secure genuine information about the Church and her teachings, was to go to headquarters—ask Catholics. When we want legal advice, we go to a lawyer; when we are ill we call in a doctor. No one would go to a Wall Street broker to have a broken leg repaired; no one would seek out an opera singer to conduct a law suit. And yet many of us formulate our ideas about the Catholic Church by consulting agnostics, theosophists, barbers and bootblacks. I was once guilty of such absurdities myself.

When, however, I began to seek information regarding Catholicism from Catholics, it was not long before I discovered that a great Catholic thinker like John Henry Newman, for instance, could tell me more about the good, the beautiful and the true, than men like Matthew Arnold, John Ruskin or Emerson could ever tell me; that the mind of a St. Augustine or a St. Thomas Aquinas made the paltry pettifogging of the average modern philosopher seem utterly puerile and piffling—and so on and so on.

Yet even that was but seeing and learning of the Church from the outside. So long as I went no further than to merely read and study Catholic literature and history and talk with Catholics only casually, my position was perhaps no more logical than that of the two men whom I have quoted. I could still picture myself as sympathizing with those who would say "that's just wish-fancy, brother; faith stuff," and so on. Still, it did bring me nearer the Church; for no normally intelligent, fairminded student of Catholic Christianity who first washes his mind of his preconceived notions, prejudices and vague fancies regarding it (and ceases giving weight to the opinions of uninformed non-Catholics) can fail to find himself ultimately rather close to the door of the Church—provided, of course, he sincerely tries to understand.

Close to the door—yes. But one never goes through the door on that alone. I mean *really* goes through. One might go into the Catholic Church on one's emotions, as some no doubt have—and perhaps soon come out again. But to really go in, one needs more than mere cold knowledge of facts; more than even a complete knowledge of doctrine or dogma; and certainly more than exalted emotion. One must, as Cardinal Newman long ago put it, "make a venture"; seek and accept that which is God-given—the gift of faith.

The gift of faith! That brings us right back to the remark of my smoker companion, "faith stuff; you imagine things," and so on. But that's just where the Catholic parts company with the sceptic. The sceptic says, "Good night, brother," and fades out when you begin to explain to him that Catholics believe certain objective truths—metaphysical truths—which are beyond the capacity of natural human reason—supernatural truths. Usually he will not wait long enough to be told that belief in the supernatural, as well as the natural, is the cornerstone of true Christianity; that the Catholic Church teaches and has always taught that Christianity would be the veriest nonsense if there were no supernatural order. But he hastens away before he gets in too deep, as did my companion on the train.

It was about the Catholic doctrine of the supernatural that I was reading on the train in that "mystery" story. As every informed Catholic knows, the supernatural mysteries are not explained by the findings of natural science; they are in the field not of the physical but of the metaphysical. Natural law is true in its own sphere, the natural order; and we grasp it through natural reason. But the supernatural is primarily apprehended through God-given faith. Of course the existence of God as well as some of His attributes are apprehended by natural human intelligence through the evidences of nature. As St. Paul put it, "The invisible things of Him, from the creation of the world, are clearly seen, being understood by the things that are made;

His eternal power also, and His divinity." But full knowledge of God and of His intentions towards men comes to us as revealed truth through the supernatural gift of faith. And this gift of faith comes to us in only one way—through the action of divine grace on the souls of men.

In my old days of scepticism and ignorance I called all this self-delusion; I was one with the chap who said "faith stuff; you imagine things." Then I was blind; but now I see. I see because I finally made that venture of faith which every man must make if he hopes ever to grasp the meaning of the supernatural. And I do not hesitate to say to any sceptic that if he but first try, honestly and sincerely, to recognize the limitations of his own pygmy intellect, and then—having crushed his pride to that extent—undertakes sincerely to make the "venture" of faith, he will soon become conscious of the fact that something "supernatural" is happening to *him*.

That, and that alone, will mark his true entry into the Church. He will now be on the inside. And as I found to be the case myself, he will soon experience a sense of peace and certainty of which he had no conception before. He will find himself no longer mentally and spiritually "static," but growing all the time, learning more of truth and beauty all the time. The Faith will open and develop like a flower, as he progresses in knowledge of it and of its practice. And he will soon begin to wonder at the paltry notions of life he formerly held. He will indeed wonder why he had been so slow in grasping eternal truth.

And so it is that when, nowadays, people say to me, "It's a mystery how a man of your intelligence and lifelong experience—hard-headed—hard-boiled—" can fall for "faith stuff," the one sure answer I can give them is that, coöper-

ating with divine grace, I made my "venture," thereby receiving this God-given gift of faith.

2.

Some years after I had left all my vain fancies behind me
and had embraced the Catholic Faith, the following message of good will came to me from a Protestant clergyman
friend who had but just learned of my change. His comment brings to the front certain things which bear on the
whole problem of the Christian Faith.

"I am ready to rejoice with you that you have found the
pearl of great price," he wrote; "that you have reached
'home,' and are now happy in the blessings of peace, security, order and truth. But there are, as you must know,
many of us who share these same blessings with you, even
though 'home' to us may not be within the sheltering fold
of the Roman Catholic Church."

In this same letter he went on to explain his own ideas
of what constituted a religious home. He contended that
it need not necessarily be a home in any Christian communion; that there is truth to be found in all religions, and
one may be happy in the blessings of peace, security, order
and truth in any of them, "for the various religions of mankind are merely different paths all leading to the same goal."

Naturally as a Catholic I had some comment to make on
that point of view. I readily agreed that many men are and
can be in good faith in almost any religion; that there are
to be found elements of truth—Catholic truth—in practically every religion, as well as in every philosophy or ethi-
cal system worthy of mention. But I wondered why he, a
professed Christian preacher, placed a revealed religion like

Christianity in the same category with the various "natural" religions of mankind. Was he not supposed to teach, as a spokesman of his Church, that Christianity is a divinely revealed religion proclaimed by the God-man, Christ Jesus —and therefore not to be classed with mere man-made religions?

Of course I knew his answer in advance. He did not believe in the Incarnation. He viewed it as "an engaging myth, though with valuable symbolic implications." What that may mean anyone can determine for himself. But that the divine Incarnation is nowadays denied in many quarters, is a familiar fact to us all. All the way from modernist Anglicanism, along the ever-widening road of "liberalism," we find this to be the fact. And of course, wherever traditional Christian dogma of this kind has been lopped off, the reality of the supernatural has become less and less apparent to men. Which reminds me of an incident of recent date.

Talking with an old "liberalist" minister, I said something about the sacrament of baptism. He said to me, "I've never been present at a baptism myself, but I suppose the Catholics and Episcopalians and some other sects still practice it. It's one of the old superstitions which don't die out." I ventured to suggest that the sacrament of baptism was instituted by Christ Himself. "Perhaps," he said; "but you see, I don't believe in the divinity of Christ." Asking him if he had ever believed in Christ's divinity he replied, "Yes, as a youth I used to; my parents were New England puritans. But later I came to feel, with men like Emerson, that it is a myth." I asked him what he did believe; did he believe in the existence of God, for instance? This was his reply: "If you mean a personal God, I say no, very positively. But there may be, must be, some power or force back of the universe; that I grant. Just what it is, I don't know. Science, I suppose, will explain it all some day. In the meanwhile, according to my view, the best we Christian ministers can do is to preach good morals and good works."

That is just one concrete example of how Christian dogma has been progressively lopped off in certain circles of non-Catholic Christianity. I would not imply that this is wholly characteristic of Protestantism; by no means. There are large groups of Protestants who still adhere rigidly to much of the teaching of Christ, who have not lost the conception of the supernatural, who do still believe in the divine Incarnation. But this seems far less so than was the case a generation or two ago. Many modern people, whether they class themselves as Christians or not, seem to be conscious or unconscious followers of the pragmatic philosophy widely popularized by William James during my own young manhood. Truth, according to this philosopher, is really nothing but subjective human fancy working in the mind or emotions of the individual. If it fails to "work," it should be discarded for some other fancy which will "work." He asserted, for example, that it is all right for you to believe in the existence of a God if it makes you feel good to do so. But if such belief seems to give you no comfort, then there is no truth for you in the idea that a God exists. Which means, of course, that the existence of God is only a wish-fancy, and in no sense an objective reality.

Now when I lived in that intellectual atmosphere—as I did for many years—even though I tried to force myself to be content with this pragmatic view of truth and of God, I was, as a matter of fact, always unsettled and dissatisfied and ever on the lookout for "something better"; for some improvement on these nebulous religious notions.

To yearn for something better than a nebulous type of religious belief surely is commendable. The unrest of myself and of those who thought along the same lines is easily understandable. And right here may be the place to ask (having in mind the limpid phrase of my kindly modernist well wisher, who had obviously lost all belief in Christian supernaturalism)—just where *do* the blessings of peace, security, order and truth come in, in this broad field of religious doubt and uncertainty?

The sure answer is—as I can myself well attest—they do *not* come in. And that fact was one of the major reasons why I long ago said good-by to it all and tossed overboard this pragmatic philosophy. There were never to be found any blessings of peace, security, order and truth in any neck of these woods that I had explored.

3.

But are these blessings to be found in their fullness in *any* field of religion? That I can answer with conviction. They are indeed—in the Catholic religion.

It is often remarked that the sincerely practicing Catholic seems to possess, or at least lives as though he did possess, some mysterious secret. "These Catholics; they are so serenely sure," is a remark one often hears. They appear to be oddly happy and at peace in their religion, often regardless of their vicissitudes, such as poor health, financial misfortune and other difficulties; matters which hound the lives of many. And it is frequently asked, "How can this be? Have the Catholics got something the rest of us haven't got?"

Most decidedly the Catholic has "got" something. He has a divinely revealed religion; a religion he can grasp and believe with certitude; a religion he can get his teeth into. He finds himself standing on solid rock, not on shifting sands. Misgivings as to the profound truth of his Faith never assail him; he does not need to puzzle over conflicting views nor work himself into a fever of unrest by watching out for "something better," for from the very depth of his soul he believes there is nothing better. Ignorant though he may sometimes be of the finer points of dogma; incapable though he may be of verbally refuting all the attacks on the Faith which come his way, of certain fundamentals he is never ignorant. He believes, for instance, that truth is objective; that truth is unchanging; that truth is one; that God is supreme Truth. And being convinced of at least that, and regardless of his inability to lucidly answer all criticisms of his faith, he is always happy in the blessings of peace, security, order and truth, insofar as his religious life is concerned.

That's the way it "works" with the sincerely believing Catholic. And that is the way it has "worked" with me since those days, now far back at the beginning of the last decade, when, to use the words of G. K. Chesterton, I began "to behold with astonishment and enthusiasm a Divine Company and a Divine Captain:" when I "was not left alone with the Inner Light, but definitely recognized an outer light, fair as the sun, clear as the moon, terrible as an army with banners." In other words, when at last I turned to look outwards in search of the truth of things as they are, and no longer wasted time looking inward at my own vain fancies.

Let me be a little more explicit about this—even at the risk of repetition. Christianity in its modern garb had landed me nowhere; neither had modern philosophy, nor any of the popular non-Christian cults—theosophy and other pantheistic notions the least of all. But when at last I turned to the Catholic Church and seriously undertook to examine without prejudice her claim that she speaks with the infallible authority of Jesus Christ, it was not very long before I began to see a great light. That great light was the light of the supernatural. I was slowly but surely, as I went on with my studies and researches, grasping the significance of Christianity as a supernaturally revealed religion; something I had never clearly comprehended before. But now, as the supernatural light of divine truth increasingly pervaded my mind, I *was* beginning to understand.

4.

To begin to understand, however, is not enough; one must go further, make one's "venture" and seek the gift of faith. Perhaps I can throw a little light on that point by citing an incident of my pre-Catholic days. Having acquired something of an understanding, I still did not fully believe; I still had to make my "venture," and therefore had not completely grasped the truth.

It happened that I went to a midnight Mass on Christmas Eve. The church was ablaze with lights as I entered; a long procession of priests, acolytes and choristers in colorful vestments were moving into the sanctuary. There were strains of heavenly music. And then, as I was crowded for-

ward into a seat, the mystery of Bethlehem was being proclaimed from the altar—"Christ is born to us; come let us
adore Him!"

Could I believe that? Had God really become a little
child? Had the Infinite been born of a Virgin and wrapped
in swaddling clothes and laid in a manger? My ingrained
scepticism cried aloud that it was preposterous.

And yet the happy faces of the hundreds around me
proved that they certainly believed it to be true. Was I the
only sceptic there? I wondered; and as I glanced from face
to face, seeing the joy of faith in every countenance, a
guilty feeling crept through me. Why, with my persisting
scepticism, had I desecrated this holy place on this holy
night?

But despite this lingering scepticism, this midnight Mass
moved me deeply. I departed in a meditative mood, but
with the war of doubt still fighting within. For many
months now I had known that the entire Christian structure
(which I had long been studying for a fuller understanding) depended for its truth on this basic fact of Bethlehem.
If this were true; if the little child born that night and
adored as the Messias, was really God Himself, the God-
man, the Word made flesh—then every dogma of the Catholic Church was true, for they all hung directly on this one
supernatural divine event.

But was it true? . . . In time I got the answer. It *was*
true! The Babe of Bethlehem was indeed the Divine Son
of God, the Second Person of the Holy Trinity.

How did I come to believe that? In only one way—
through revelation. It is only through His revelation,
through God-given faith in revealed truth, that anyone can
come to believe with understanding. True it is that through

natural reason we logically prove God's existence; all the evidences of nature prove that. But the evidences of nature alone do not bring the God of revelation down to us for our full apprehension and love. Only revealed truth, as illuminated to us by divine grace, can do that.

For years I have carried in my memory some eloquent lines on the reality of God, which are to be found in a summary on the first page of a compilation of Cardinal Newman's principal writings, issued a number of years ago.[1] To me these brief paragraphs give a wonderfully vivid and accurate vision of the greatness of God, as He is understood by the teachings of Catholic Christianity. They seem to sum up the foundation of the Faith. From memory I quote them in full.

God's existence is immediately and irrefutably disclosed as soon as we open our eyes to life as it really is; against the background of life's beginning and ending, God appears without beginning and without end; against the background of its helpless dependence, God appears, whose Being alone is self-grounded; against the background of its limitations and divisions, God appears—Infinite Perfection; God, the divine Majesty.

But it is in the experience of a tender and reverent conscience that we hear, as it were, His voice addressing us personally; that He, in our experience of guilt, remorse and penance increasingly reveals Himself as the transcendent ground of all morality, the supreme Lawgiver, commanding good and forbidding evil; the strict inflexible Judge, the mighty, pure, infinite Holiness which strikes our hearts with awe. . . . But in spite of all this, there is a voice of infinite mercy: "Come to Me." . . .

[1] *A Newman Synthesis,* arranged by Rev. Erich Przywara, S.J., Longmans, Green & Co., New York, 1931.

Thus His image grows with the actual development of our interior life ever mightier, without limit. And the more we apprehend Him, the more does He elude our grasp, so that it is precisely in the realization that our quest can never reach its goal that we attain our profoundest knowledge of Him as the infinite and incomprehensible. And nevertheless, precisely *as* the infinite and incomprehensible, He is our God, and "our heart is restless until it rests in Him."

Men may conjure up imaginative notions of God, as do the pantheists, theosophists and nature worshippers, picturing Him as an immanent, pervading influence or an unknown, faraway force or mysterious power behind or within the universe; they may picture Him as abstract retributive justice or as mechanistic cause and effect, arbitrary and relentless in a merciless iron law or Karma; but only through the Christian Revelation can we come to know God the Almighty Creator of the universe, as not only the strictly inflexible Judge, but as also a God of infinite mercy and infinite love for His creatures. A God whose love for us so far transcends our human conception of love, that it is to us inevitably veiled in mystery—as in the great mystery of the Holy Trinity; and also in that great supernatural mystery of the Incarnation—the mystery of the birth of the Babe of Bethlehem, when "the Word was made flesh, and came and dwelt among us."

5.

It is certainly true that thousands of men and women who are not members of the Catholic Church, believe in the God of Revelation and in the Divinity of Christ, despite the modernist dilutions of the orthodox Christian Faith so popular with many. We find many nuggets of truth in all non-Catholic Christian groups, as well as in various natural religions. But all the genuine truth found in these fields is Catholic truth. It is frequently torn, however, from its original and true context by private judgment and various human fancies. All experience proves that wherever men try to pick the wheat from the chaff by their own private judgment, fancies and prejudices enter in to distort the meaning. Truth is in danger of being broken up, of perhaps becoming half-truth, or of being placed in contexts which destroy or limit its significance and meaning. And one is soon lost in confusions and contradictions.

If, however, Christianity is understood as a religion re-vealed to mankind by God Himself, and that the Church which His divine Son founded on the rock of Peter to preach this revelation to all mankind, speaks with His un-erring authority, then we have certitude—but only then.

Thus it became logically clear to me that only by means of an infallible authority for correct interpretation could the Scriptures be relied on as a firm basis for Christian be-liefs. This was the attitude of the Catholic Church when she first gave the Gospels to the world, and that is her atti-tude today. She does not tell you and me to puzzle over the meanings of Scriptural texts, to pick and choose, ac-cording to our own bias and fancies, from the traditional teachings of the Church. She, the infallible guardian of God's revelation, explains these truths to you and to me.

The great St. Augustine said in the fifth century, "I might not be able to believe the Gospels, did not the Cath-olic Church move me to." That had always seemed to me a "hard saying," even an absurdity, before I had examined, with an open mind, the Catholic evidences and proofs. But now I could only see it as a wise saying, full of significance. For I had come to see that the voice of the Catholic Church is none other than the voice of Christ Himself.

6.

And so it was that I came upon the *true* pearl of great price. Having definitely grasped the revealed truth that the Babe of Bethlehem was indeed the Incarnate God, my full journey to the Catholic Church was inevitable and assured.

There could be no further doubt for me. As Christ had founded this visible Church on earth, choosing Peter as her head; as He had sent His Holy Spirit to guard His Church from error in teaching faith and morals, and had promised to be with His Church until the end of time—it was crystal clear to me that His Church must have had a continuous history throughout the centuries, must still be living in the world, must still be one in unity of doctrine and of jurisdiction; and her teachings in the field of faith and morals must still be the same as at the beginning, and as sure and true as when Christ first proclaimed them.

Now the only Christian Church on earth which in any way fits in with this description—or indeed makes any similar claims—is this One, Holy, Catholic and Apostolic Roman Church.

CHAPTER THREE

THE SEASONING PROCESS

I.

LEAVING BEHIND one's former non-Catholic life is but one side of a conversion experience; the other side consists not alone of one's acceptance of Catholic truth, but also of the process of growth into the new life which now begins. Therefore, interesting as it may be to learn of the way one had approached the Faith, it should be equally interesting to see how the convert adjusts himself to it all as time goes on.

Have you ever traveled in a slow, uncomfortable train on a long, wearisome journey; a journey which you were sure would end at a destination you had pictured in your mind as bleak and forbidding? And then, when at last you did arrive at this destination in a state of exhaustion and depression, you were relieved and overjoyed at the delightful aspect confronting you—its atmosphere of restfulness and peace?

Something like that was what I experienced when entering the Catholic Church more than ten years ago; quite unexpected and joyous surprise at what I found awaiting me. I had indeed been disturbed by misgivings. Not doctrinal doubts or difficulties; for even though the deeper meanings of the Faith would not be grasped in their fullness for many days to come—being still but vaguely apprehended—there were surely no doctrinal doubts obstructing my path. But I had long been worrying about the probable difficulties of adjusting myself to the rules and discipline of that yet mysterious thing, the Catholic way of life. Among other matters I was carrying in my mind disturbing fears of things like daily prayer requirements, early risings, frequent confessions, awful curbs on one's moral conduct—and God knows what!

A challenge indeed for a coddled, self-centered pagan whose main preoccupation for years had been the seeking of personal ease and comfort. More than once had I been warned by non-Catholics that while the Catholic Church might be a consoling place in which to die, it was sure to prove a bleak, forbidding and difficult place in which to live. Consequently, although I intended to try to live as a good Catholic should, I honestly dreaded what I supposed was ahead for me. I was sure I was in for a struggle for a long time to come, and was endeavoring to steel myself for the trial.

All of which was utterly absurd. I realized this before I had been a month in the Church. For while it did quite naturally take me time to settle, from the very beginning a joyous sense of freedom and release tempered all my problems and perplexities. I was gloriously aware of a distinct release from slavery—that slavery to mental confusion, doubt and uncertainty, which had held me as in a vise for years. And, as time rolled on, this awareness of freedom and release steadily increased as I came to more fully understand and absorb the deeper meanings of the Faith.

At the same time, even though one does at once find freedom and rejoices in a sense of release, one is really embarking on a voyage of discovery when entering the Catholic Church. At first, even though welcomed into his new environment with open arms, the convert is sure to feel strange—it is all "so different." If he lives in a more or less pagan environment, where Catholic converts are usually viewed as brainstorm victims, he is only too likely, for a time at least, to feel like a lone voice crying in the wilderness. For most of those around him or close to him will not take his Catholicity seriously at all; and while, in response to their continuous ridicule or tiresome incredulity, he may try to defend or explain his Catholic beliefs, he is all too conscious of the fact that he is, if not stirring up opposition and resentment, at any rate wasting his time.

He must learn, however, to take all this as a matter of course—even though so many do persist in viewing his new Catholic life as nothing but superstitious worshipping of images, fingering of beads, lighting of candles, eating fish dinners and running to confession. God help him at this stage if he happens to be short in his sense of humor!

But if he feels like a voice crying in the wilderness of his non-Catholic environment, he is also likely at first to feel like a lost soul within the Catholic body. This is particularly likely if he happens to have no close Catholic friends—lay Catholics who, perhaps, are converts themselves, or at least have sympathetic understanding of converts. There are many Catholics who do not understand converts; many who seem puzzled by the fact that you have become one of them.

Still, all this should not upset any convert for long. The easy remedy is to seek out sympathetic Catholics and make friends with them as fast as you can. This circumstance of not knowing many Catholics didn't depress me outstandingly, for my lonesomeness was tempered by the relief I felt in leaving a world of painfully boring emptiness of worthwhile interests. This was so despite the fact that it took me some time to fill my mind with a full understanding of Catholic truth. In any event, the latter process is liable to keep one preoccupied and busy for a considerable period; especially if one has a taste for study. Although I had already read scores of standard Catholic books, I found it well worth while to read a great many more after I got into the Church to further clarify my understanding.

But it is often the case that despite his eagerness to adjust himself to the Catholic way of life, the new convert can scarcely avoid continuing for a time to react to many things in a non-Catholic way. He does find it hard to abruptly break off his old pagan habits. It calls for real heroism, for instance, for him to abandon his lifelong habit of lying abed mornings in pleasing anticipation of a hot breakfast in the next room or just around the corner, and instead, to emerge into the cold street on a winter morning bound for an early Mass. That may be easy for the seasoned Catholic; he has probably been doing it since boyhood. But for an erstwhile lazy pagan like myself, it was a strenuous act of self-discipline—even though I had never in the past found it difficult to submit to an early rising if headed for a day on the golf course!

However, this struggle to beat the sunrise on cold winter mornings is soon tempered by one's joy in finding churches thronged while the pagan world is still asleep; and one's happiness in being one of these thousands of practicing Catholics grows apace. And the habit grows; with some it becomes a daily habit. I know more than one Catholic who would no more miss his morning Mass—barring sickness—than he would miss going to business that day.

2.

To me it was a new experience to find churches always well filled, regardless of the hour, of weather conditions or of the season. Coming out of a Protestant environment, where I had never known any church to be crowded except at the main service on Sunday, or on special occasions when fine music or a strong preacher were the drawing cards, I was enormously impressed by the full congregations always to be found in Catholic churches. And even more impressive was the fact that such large numbers of the faithful regularly approached the altar rail to receive Holy Communion. I had of course known that there were many frequent and some daily as well as weekly communicants in the Catholic Church, but only now did I begin to realize that there were thousands in all large population centers.

A Protestant clergyman of my acquaintance, who was unusually successful in filling his own church by his pulpit eloquence, was inclined to dispute my statement that the Catholic church just around the corner had ten times as many attendants as his church had on Sundays. "Why," he exclaimed, "my church is packed to the doors; every seat filled every Sunday. And you know we can seat almost as many people as your big Catholic church can."

"That may be so," I replied; "but you have but one main service on Sunday mornings. The Catholic church around the corner has seven Masses on Sundays, the first at six o'clock; and at every Mass the church is practically full. The same is true of all the Catholic churches in this town; in every town."

In fact, one of the things which at first amazes more than

one convert, if he happens to live in a large city, is the
spectacle on Sunday mornings of great throngs of people
emerging from church when he is just going in. Usually,
when one Mass is over, the next one immediately begins.

The novelty of this world of full and consistent church
attendance is not, however, confined to the great numbers
the convert sees at Masses. It is not so much the size of the
congregations that impresses him; rather is it their character. Wherever he goes to Mass, he sees people from every
walk of life; some in silks and fine linen, some more modestly attired, and some practically in rags and tatters. The
rich, the moderately well-to-do, the struggling poor, the
dull witted as well as the mentally brilliant—they are all
here. Old and young, prosperous and poverty-stricken, the
admired as well as the ignored by the world outside, all
rub shoulders, all kneel together at the altar rail, all worship
as one. To me it was a benediction the first time I saw it.
As the long sanctuary rail filled again and again with devout
men, women and children, all so reverent in the reception
of the divine Eucharistic food for their souls, my joy and
gratitude in having at last been led to the Faith were quite
overflowing.

And now, for the first time perhaps, I began dimly to
understand why the true Catholic so ardently and de-
votedly loves his great Mother, the Church. That indeed,
is one of the things which it takes time for the convert to
learn. He cannot grasp its meaning from the outside; mere
looking on is of little help. He must be in it and a part of
it—have some experience himself—before he can fully
know the answer.

The answer is of course (at least partially) because the
Church is so *catholic*. She embraces all and she treats all

alike; her unity and solidarity extend into every walk of life, and she brings with it all a sanctity which can nowhere else be found. Not that her members are all endowed with sanctity. This great universal organism includes both saints and sinners. As our Blessed Lord proclaimed, the Church is a field sown with good wheat, but among which grow up tares as well. And her tragedy has been, throughout all the ages, that the tares threaten constantly to choke the good wheat.

But her whole mission is to sanctify her children, and the standards she raises and the rules she makes are alike for all, whether they be rich or poor, high or low, ignorant or educated, privileged or unprivileged. She never requires one sinner to rise to a higher moral standard than another; she merely asks all to be penitent, that they all strive and desire to live better lives. She offers nothing to the saint that she does not offer to the sinner.

Moreover, she well understands the human heart and its weaknesses, and while she never lowers her standards for anyone, her patience with weak humanity is inexhaustible —like the patience of a good mother with her wayward children. Most of us slip more or less from our moorings now and then, but the arms of the Church are ever open to give us "another chance."

Her sanctity grows out of the holiness of the means she brings to her children to strengthen and cleanse them. The remedy she has is the same for all—the imparting of the life of grace to the soul. This is one of the great secrets which explain the deep love of her faithful children for her. Like her Divine Founder, she is in very truth the friend of publicans and sinners, and her mission is to bring them all, if she can, into her life-supernatural, her communion of saints.

To the average person of Protestant or pagan heritage there is perhaps nothing so difficult to understand, in the fullness of meaning, as the Catholic teaching of the perfect and indivisible union of Christ and His Church. It is at first a startling thing to him to be told that this visible organism on earth speaks with the infallible authority of Jesus Christ. Moreover, it is quite certain to be a difficulty for any non-Catholic, when approaching the Church, to fully abandon what has been a lifelong habit of relying on private judgment in interpreting the Scriptures, and in particular the teachings of Christ and His Apostles.

That, however, is precisely what he must do—wholly abandon dependence on his own or other men's individual judgment in this respect. He must clearly recognize that the Church herself speaks with the authority of Christ in the whole field of faith and morals, for she is not a mere man-made institution formulated and held together by ordinary human agreement, but is a divine organism founded by Christ Himself.

Right here might be mentioned one of the reasons why, now and then, we see a convert (or lax, cradle Catholic) fall away from the Church. It is usually the case that this person has never clearly understood the meaning of the divinity of the Church. That was the case with a certain lapsed Catholic I knew all about. First a Protestant, then a poorly instructed Catholic who evidently never fully absorbed Catholic teaching; then a Protestant once more; and finally, after a few further years of uncertainty and unsettlement, an unhappy sceptic wandering from pillar to post, trying one futile philosophy after another, but no-where finding peace.

3.

Perhaps the most difficult thing for the new convert to accustom himself to, is "frequenting" the Sacrament of Penance. He finds it hard to go to confession. Unless it happens that he has come out of the High Episcopal Church, where the practice of hearing confessions prevails with some, it is an entirely new experience. The timidity and self-consciousness with which some new converts approach the confessional box is, I suppose, quite puzzling to many a Catholic who has been doing it all his life. But with the newcomer, it may be his first experience in breaking down his pagan pride.

Still, even the most timid get over this obsession of fear and trembling after a little experience. I recall that after my first few months in the Church, I no longer bothered to formulate my own confessions in a cloud of words, designed to make my sins sound less shocking to myself or to the priest. I quickly discovered that you can neither confuse nor shock the priest; he brushes your verbiage aside and forces you to the point. And so I soon stopped this waste of words, plumped out briefly what I had to say—and felt better for it.

Confession is of course anonymous unless one wants it otherwise; and while at first it may seem an awful ordeal, one soon comes to love this privilege of regular contacts with a good confessor. And the counsel, the unraveling of perplexing problems, both spiritual and temporal, are not the least of the benefits derived from also having a regular spiritual director or advisor.

Non-Catholics often wonder why apparently sinless people go so frequently to confession. What can they possibly have on their consciences? And many a new and unseasoned convert will also wonder at this at first. He may not be in the habit of committing many grievous or even mild sins, and yet he is told that the custom of going to weekly, or at least semi-monthly confession, has very great merit. But why?

The answer is simple. The Sacrament of Penance, next to the Sacrament of the Holy Eucharist, is the most important sacrament in the daily life of the Catholic. It is the method by which sanctifying grace is restored to the penitent when his sins are confessed and he has made a good act of contrition. If he has committed no mortal sins, but is guilty of minor or venial sins only, he has not completely lost sanctifying grace, although it may have been weakened in his soul. The Sacrament of Penance, however, will increase this grace, and that is why the moral state of the penitent is strengthened by "going to confession"—just as it is also strengthened when he receives Holy Communion.

And the rewards are immeasurable. I have invariably noticed, during all my years in the Church, that the person who goes regularly to confession with the right disposition and intention, and is a frequent communicant—thus keeping close to the Sacraments—displays in a marked degree that "peace which passes understanding." You see it in his face; you detect it in his daily life. For that person is living close to the supernatural.

4.

As the convert settles down in his new home, an unknown world is really opening before him. For one thing, unless he has already had some insight into the Catholic world, he is sure to be surprised at the extent of the apostolic activities of both the clergy and laity. He may have already known that the Church embraces many Orders of priests, nuns and other religious, entirely aside from the diocesan clergy; but he probably had very crude and limited notions of their purposes and activities. For instance, he is almost certain to have had some very absurd notions regarding the Jesuits. I surely did, having read in my youth many devastating stories about them. But now, as a Catholic, I was soon reading a true history of the Society of Jesus, as well as accurate and absorbing lives of St. Ignatius Loyola and St. Francis Xavier; and particularly, I recall, lives of those other remarkable men of the days of the Counter-reformation, St. Peter Canisius, St. Francis Borgia, St. Robert Bellarmine and so on. Moreover, I was discovering a vast world of modern Jesuit activity of a most apostolic kind.

And I also began to discover the Benedictines, Dominicans, Franciscans and Capuchins, Paulists, Passionists, Redemptorists, the Maryknoll Fathers and Sisters and many other Orders, all at work in many ways and in different parts of the world, and I was astounded at the extent and scope of their activities. As for the many Orders of nuns—why, they were "all over the place"; literally scores of distinct Orders, which I immediately tried to classify and count by their differences in costume—a hopeless task for any mere man!

It is indeed a vast, pulsating world the convert has entered. Catholic lay Action looms up before him in a hundred forms; perhaps he had had no previous idea of the extensive activities of the laity. Invitations soon fly to him to "join up," to "do your bit," to write articles, to make speeches. Moreover, there are all sorts of societies, clubs and sodalities in all cities and indeed in all sizeable parishes; nearly always a St. Vincent de Paul Society and a Holy Name Society for men—not to mention national organizations such as the National Council of Catholic Men, and so on. The newcomer may or may not fit into all of these activities; this depends upon his age, resources or personal circumstances. But they are there for him to choose from.

And now, perhaps for the first time, he discovers a flood of Catholic papers and periodicals, few of which he has ever seen before. And to his surprise (especially in centers of large population) he discovers Catholic bookstores, lending libraries and reading rooms, which he could never seem to locate until he got into the Church. An even greater surprise (at least it was for me) is his discovery that there are facilities available for laymen to make spiritual retreats, just as do the priests and all other religious.

If you are an average person you will find yourself soon getting involved in activities carried on by the laity, some perhaps very congenial to you, some possibly unfitted for you at this early stage in your Catholic life. When you first planned to become a Catholic you may have had the notion that you would be "getting out of things," and would now enjoy a period of rest and relaxation. But you were wrong; you will scarcely avoid involving yourself in some activity —unless you are that odd sort of person, a recluse. As for myself, I was promptly drawn into a Convert's League and a Catholic Study Club, and at least one sodality; and being somewhat of a scribbler and amateur speaker, found myself rashly writing Catholic "literature" and making speeches before I had been in the Church six months. And I am still at it, you see!

Seasoned Catholics surely have good reasons for being bored by the chatter of the raw convert, in view of the trivial stuff most of us inflict on them. Now that I am much further along the road, my early loquacity seems absurd. I like to forget that first green year or two, when I so glibly told the world all about Catholicism, and was only in the kindergarten myself.

Yet I suppose it is only fair to make allowances for the grotesque contortions of the militant new convert. He is, in these first days of his novel and radiant rejoicing, quite naturally carried off his feet. This is evidenced by the convert-making fever which at once possesses him. He is thrilled at finding the truth and is wildly eager to impart it to others. He cannot rest until he has proclaimed it to at least all those whose friendship he values; it seems utterly selfish to keep it all to himself.

Certainly, if he is anything like I was at that time, he simply must take it for granted that all his relatives and friends will lose no time in following him in. In fact, he is likely to envisage a great company of potential converts flocking to him from over the horizon; and perhaps he makes lists of these potential victims of his feverish zeal. At least that is what I did not fail to do.

I had scarcely started my own Catholic life when my convert-making fever was brought to white heat by receipt of a kindly letter of congratulation from a saintly priest— Father James B. Hayden, of Schenectady, New York. He

enclosed with his letter a little story of a distinguished
Indian Brahmin who had become a Catholic through studying the *Imitation of Christ*, and then had forthwith converted his wife and twelve children, besides over thirty
relatives and friends. Well, thought I, if a lone Brahmin
in faraway pagan India can do all that, then surely right
here in little old New York, already so largely Catholic, I
ought to do twice as well in half the time. And I had visions
of packing a dozen church pews with new and ardent
Catholics long before that first year was out.

That was of course when I was still in the clouds; before
I had come down to earth at all. I recollect that when I first
reserved a sitting in my new parish church, I played with
the idea of reserving an entire pew with a seating capacity
of a dozen. But another convert of longer standing, reading
my thought, here offered a bit of sage advice.

"You will never need more than one seat," said he.
"When I started out years ago I was sure I could convert
the whole town in short order. But in twenty years I haven't
converted a single soul as far as I know. You may think
you know a lot of prospects, and no doubt you do; the
woods are full of prospective converts. But they never become Catholics; they linger in the woods until they die.
People who actually come into the Church are usually the
sort who have always been antagonistic—or at least indifferent. For instance, I've known you for years, and you
were the last man I would ever have thought would become
interested in the Church. When I first saw you at Mass I
was sure you had just wandered in out of curiosity or by
mistake."

Food for thought. And after ten years' experience, I
know there is a lot in it. I have been told, from time to time,

that I have been instrumental in leading certain persons into the Church. But few of such known to me were ever on any prospect list of mine. They were, in practically all cases, individuals whom I had classed as quite beyond the pale. Scarcely any of my original list of hoped-for-converts ever came in. The one outstanding exception was, of course, my wife. She did come in. But I always knew that grace was working there.

True it is that another member of our family came tumbling in early; almost on my heels. This was my wife's niece, Dorothy Fremont Grant, who has since become a well-known Catholic writer and lecturer. But she was on my *hopeless* list—not my hoped-for list. She was one of those extraordinary persons who now and then surprise all and sundry by jumping in with a bound while you are looking the other way. They believe in the short road, not the long road home. You may wonder if such streamliners make good Catholics. Well, she's the proof that they sometimes do—wonderful ones.

5.

I have said much in this chapter about the reactions of the average convert to his new environment; and have also briefly explained a few points of Catholic doctrine where it seemed in order to do so. But the most fundamental side of the convert's seasoning is still to be mentioned.

It has often been said that no one can come properly into the Church except on one's knees; one must stoop to the posture of prayer. That is what I had supposed I had done; I had made a real effort to overcome my pride and acquire at least a slight degree of humility. It was therefore something of a shock to have my spiritual director say to me one day:

"You don't seem to have caught the true Catholic spirit. You must learn to see yourself, not as you like to think you are, but as you *truly* are—and then strive to live more in accordance with, and adjust your way of life to, what you truly know you should be."

I had to ask him to explain this bit of cryptic counsel; it was all too obscure to a dullard like me. And what he said in reply was the following:

"You say you wish to live the life of a good Catholic. Being a good Catholic means, above all else, to strive to be, day in and day out, a humble follower of Christ. A follower —not a mere proclaimer. Go get yourself a copy of Thomas à Kempis' *Following of Christ;* read it, study it, master it. Then you will begin to understand what I am driving at and need ask no more questions."

Most of us everyday Catholics, I imagine, give far more attention to some other virtues—prudence, for instance— than we do to the virtue of humility. Our pride and vanity, as well as our selfishness, constantly block any good intentions we may have for really following Christ. I fear that most of us are very far from a true understanding of the Catholic norm.

To live a life of true humility is, without doubt, the hardest task of all. Only the saints have learned its secret. Yet one may at least come to understand something about it —as well as about its antithesis, pride. Pride is not only the greatest obstacle to the practice of a true Catholic life; it is the primary reason why many persons will not come into the Church; they refuse to come in on their knees.

But none of us can rightly claim to be truly practicing

Catholics—true followers of Christ—unless we are willing
to merge our lives, with all our joys and sorrows, and with
both the successes and sacrifices which go to make up our
daily round of living, to the truths we accepted when embracing the Faith. For, above all else, the gift of faith is
something to be lived; not merely something to be verbally
defended.

That no doubt is the lesson of all lessons for us Catholics
to learn. And yet what poor learners most of us prove to be.
We may love to stand up and shout our faith from the
housetops—on our feet; but the thing which we may know
far less about, is living our faith—on our knees.

When once trying—rather naïvely—to persuade a lax
Catholic friend to give some thought to the practice of the
Faith and get back to the Sacraments, he violently resented
my remarks. He said to me, "You still have that old puri-
tanical Protestant habit of worrying more about your
neighbor's soul than about your own. A bit of smug pride,
I call it. Your business is to look after your own conscience,
not mine."

It was a well-deserved rebuke. In my innocence, I was
only trying to revive in his apparently lax and lukewarm
mind what, at the beginning of this chapter, is referred to
as "that yet mysterious thing, the Catholic way of life."
But of course the Catholic way of life can only be correctly
expressed by those who examine their own consciences before they undertake to tell their neighbors to examine
theirs. That is the beginning of humility.

One thing, however, I do know, after ten years of faulty
conformity with that yet mysterious thing, the Catholic
way of life. And it is this: One may acquire a full intellectual knowledge of the Catholic Faith; may even come

to know all Catholic dogma by heart—and still not be a true Catholic at all. For, as the author of the *Imitation* put it so long ago:

What avails it thee to discourse deeply of the Trinity, if thou be void of humility, and displeasing to the Trinity? . . . If thou didst know the whole Bible by heart, and the sayings of all the philosophers, what would it profit thee without the love of God and His grace?

CHAPTER FOUR

THE LIFE OF GRACE

I.

ON AN EARLIER PAGE I mentioned the fact that I had the privilege of meeting His Eminence, the late Cardinal Hayes, a month or two before being received into the Church, and that this occurred at St. Josephs, Sullivan County, New York. It might be of interest to explain the circumstances of that meeting, as it had not only a direct bearing on my subsequent reception into the Church, but also on certain other experiences relating to my later Catholic life.

As it happens, my family summer home has been for many years located in Sullivan County. We are in a small summer community known as Merriewold, a settlement primarily of New York City families, which was originally settled more than fifty years ago. It adjoins the extensive reservation owned by the Sisters of St. Dominic, where the Sisters have carried on for many years what is known as St. Josephs Mountain School, a high school for girls, as well as a grammer school for boys—and in recent years large summer camps for both boys and girls.

Within this Dominican reservation, which comprises about fifteen hundred acres, including a farm, a fresh water lake and an extensive woodland, was the summer residence of the late Cardinal; a comfortable house on the ridge not

far from the convent and school buildings. It was in this
house that the beloved Cardinal passed to his heavenly reward at the close of the summer of 1938. And today, if
you will make the journey to St. Josephs, and will take the
picturesque road which runs up a short distance beyond the
convent and through a beautiful grove of beech and pine
trees, you will come to the lovely shrine which has been
erected to the Cardinal's memory at the grotto of Our Lady
of Lourdes—a natural grotto of unusual charm, which has
been famous in this countryside for years.

To the southeast of St. Josephs, not much more than a
mile away, is our own family residence. And a little beyond
that, on the reverse shore of Merriewold Lake, a small log-
cabin nestles in the woods. This little studio camp is largely
the work of my own hands. I was born to be a carpenter,
and this small log structure—known as Camp Solitude—is
my supreme achievement as an amateur manipulator of the
hammer and the saw.

For years I have made use of this studio in the spring,
summer and autumn months, particularly when the rest of
my family are absent and the larger house is closed. In my
more youthful days I often came up here week ends in the
dead of winter, even when the road around the lake was
impassable because of the snow and ice, and the only way
to reach the camp was to cross the frozen lake.

This somewhat diminutive mountain camp is completely
equipped for simple cooking and for sleeping, and a large
fireplace is available for cold weather. Most of the furniture
and fixtures are of my own construction. It is really quite a
completely equipped literary workshop. Many a manuscript have I banged out on my typewriter here. Here it
was that I wrote *The Long Road Home*, nearly ten years

ago, and here it is that I am now busily laboring over this second book.

The sun sets directly across the little lake in the spring and summer months, and often there is at sunset a golden sheen on the gently rippling water; or, if the day is calm, the surface of the lake may look like a shining golden floor. Many a late afternoon have I seen it thus; and well do I recall just such an evening of golden sunlight one Saturday at the close of day more than ten years ago, as I rowed across the lake from the farther shore to spend the night at the camp.

It was at the time when my long mental struggles with Catholic problems and perplexities were practically over. I had at last surmounted all my doctrinal difficulties; in fact, felt quite ready to enter the Church. But unlike most of those who find themselves drawn to the Catholic Faith, I had never consulted or sought the instruction of a priest. I had been trying to instruct myself without the aid of any priest or any informed Catholic. That may sound extraordinary, but nevertheless it is a fact. Now, however, I had reached the point where the problem of how to go about "getting into" the Church was preoccupying me; had been preoccupying me in fact for months. My primary reason for this visit to the camp was to think things over alone and try to come to some decision as to what move to make next.

It happened to be an abnormally warm spell in late April; an early touch of summer weather. As I rowed across the lake in my small boat that afternoon, the sky was speckled with fleecy clouds all in a riot of color from the setting sun, which was dropping behind the western ridge. I rested on my oars to drink in this masterpiece of nature. There was perfect stillness, not a ripple on the water, not a sound from the shore. Silently I sat in that slowly drifting boat, watching the colors in the clouds as they mingled and softened.

Then suddenly across the lake came the reverberating peal of a bell. It was the evening Angelus at the convent on the hillside beyond the western shore. The words came to my lips, "The Angel of the Lord declared unto Mary"— and all the rest. And as no doubt with many who have visited the Holy Land, there arose to my mental vision that sweet Galilee countryside, where the Annunciation took place so long ago.

After the tolling of the bell had ceased, I lingered on in the drifting boat. Not only did I linger until the daylight gradually faded away, but drifted in the gathering darkness until the stars, one by one and then ten by ten or more, began to dot the sky. And all through that evening, as I watched the stars, and long after fastening my boat at the little dock and lighting my cabin lamps, the vision of the green hills of Galilee, and the shoreline of its lovely landlocked lake, remained with me. It was natural perhaps for this to be; for not many months had passed since my visit to the Holy Land, a visit which had marked the melting away of my last doubts regarding the essential truth of the Catholic Faith—although I had carried home with me many difficulties yet to solve. But I had at least come far enough to know, with Newman, that "ten thousand difficulties need not make a doubt."

The Angelus call from across the lake that evening was surely providential; for as a result of it came my decision. Having been a lone searcher for Catholic truth, with no close Catholic friends to guide or advise me, the problem of seeking admission into the Church was not only paramount but puzzling. I had thought of approaching Father

Fulton Sheen, whose writings had greatly clarified my understanding. But he lived in Washington—too far away. I had considered applying to the Jesuits at St. Francis Xavier's in Sixteenth Street, New York; but someone told me that the Jesuits interested themselves in "intellectuals" only—and I knew that didn't mean me. It was also suggested that I get in touch with the Paulists; they specialized in converts. I was indeed inclined to do this and during that winter had gone to the Paulist church on Ninth Avenue several Sunday evenings. One of these evenings, seeing a kindly looking priest standing in the rear as I was going out, I was all primed to speak with him; but just then he turned and entered a confessional box near by—and I fled! It wouldn't do to bother a priest with my small matter if he was stationed there to hear confessions.

Timidity was still my dominant trait, even though I had cherished the hope that I might be able one of those Sunday evenings, to meet Father Gillis, whose writings in the *Catholic World* had greatly edified me. But he was not in the church. I recollect asking one of the ushers where I might find him. He suggested that I inquire at the Paulist house on 59th Street. But I timidly sidestepped that suggestion, fearing I might have to pull him out of bed at that late hour—nine o'clock!

Yes, absurd as it now seems, my urgent desire to meet Father Gillis was hamstrung by my timidity. I say it now seems absurd, because for many years since that timorous time I have been one of the happy lay children of this gentle, saintly and truly rational priest. He has taught me so much and clarified my mind on so many aspects of Catholic truth, that I am very sure I would often have been lost without his counsel.

However, I had continued to hesitate, procrastinate, as that winter wore on, until here at last, in my little camp during that meditation on the Annunciation in far-away Galilee, the answer to my problem burst upon me as suddenly as had the ringing of the Angelus that evening. Why! St. Josephs convent chapel was of course the place for me to be received.

I slept soundly and at great peace that night. And the next morning I arose early and after a hurried breakfast went over to the Sunday Mass, with the firm resolve to seek out the chaplain for a talk.

Odd as it may seem, up to that time I knew practically nothing about the St. Josephs community. I had gone over to the chapel for Mass many times; but I knew scarcely any of the local Catholics, none of the Sisters, and had never even seen the Mother Superior. Nor did I know the chaplain; nor that Cardinal Hayes had his summer home here and often came here. I was an utter stranger; and yet I had been living in that neighborhood during the summers for more than twenty years.

This Sunday morning, however, immediately the Mass was over, I sought out the chaplain—Monsignor Vincent Arcese. He knew of me as one of the neighbors at Merriewold, but we had never met. Quite naturally he was taken by surprise when I told him of my interest in the Catholic Church; he had not previously thought of me in that connection at all. But he was most cordial. We had a long talk that day and another shortly thereafter. And then, to my surprise and delight, he invited me to come over and meet the Cardinal, who was expected up for a brief stay the following week.

That is how it came about that I had the privilege of

meeting and talking at length with Cardinal Hayes, some weeks before my reception into the Church; an event which occurred right there.

2.

As I glance back across the years to that April Sunday when I first talked with the Cardinal and told him how I had instructed myself in Catholic doctrines, I cannot avoid an inward smile. For my self-acquired knowledge was, after all, quite chaotic and incomplete. The facts of the matter were that I had been straining my eyes and taxing my brain for a considerable period over the *Summas* of St. Thomas Aquinas, as well as a quantity of other books on Thomistic philosophy, and also quite a lot of St. Augustine. I had read many standard Catholic books, including much of Newman, and had made a somewhat extended study of church history, though without much order or system. I had also plunged into books on mysticism, such as E. I. Watkin's *Philosophy of Mysticism*—more confusing than enlightening at that particular juncture. And so my Catholic education was oddly uneven; although after puzzling over difficult dogmas for many months, I had succeeded in harmonizing them to my satisfaction. And luckily, I had well before this reached solid ground in definitely grasping the significance of the Papal supremacy.

Surely I had accomplished considerable. Confused as my mind was on many things, I had at least avoided falling into heresies. But as for being able to lucidly explain all Catholic doctrines (even to myself) or supply the correct answers to numerous questions which might be put to me by intelligent critics, or even ordinary inquirers—why, it seems to me, as I now look back, that I really knew nothing at all. Had someone asked me to explain the Catholic doctrine of grace, for instance, I can easily imagine how I would have fumbled the ball! Nor would I have been able to convincingly explain the doctrine of indulgences.

Yet I then had the assurance to tell the Cardinal that I was quite ready to step right into the Church, assuming of course, that I was proving this readiness when quoting volubly from books like Duschene's *Early Church History*, fresh in my mind from recent reading; and waxing eloquent over St. Thomas and St. Augustine. And when he finally said, "You surely are a student," I was quite sure he would receive me on the spot. However, after I had disgorged all this mighty wisdom, the Cardinal glanced up at me with his kindly smile, and with a twinkle in his eye, quietly asked, "How far have you gone in the catechism?"

The catechism? Why the catechism? Of course I had gone through the catechism; but alas, in only a streamline fashion. Nothing more had seemed necessary to me. Was I not far beyond this elementary instruction? Quite sure I was that the catechism was designed only for children and the simple-minded; not for a deep student, such as I must have proved myself to the Cardinal to be!

Some years after entering the Church I read the story of the famous convert of a century ago, Orestes A. Brownson, in which was described his first interview with Bishop Fitzpatrick of Boston. Dr. Brownson had reasoned himself into the Catholic Faith without ever having consulted a priest, just as had been the case with me. When he finally went to the bishop to tell him he wished to be received, the bishop had listened for an hour or two to his quite unique reasoning, and then had suggested that he must study and master the catechism before he could be received. Evidently Dr. Brownson's pride in his own self-acquired knowledge was very potent, for he was profoundly offended and left the bishop, inwardly fuming with indignation. But the story goes that after a few days he returned, having in the meanwhile acquired a bit of humility.

With me, however, the outcome was slightly different. Perhaps I was more conscious of my ignorance than Dr. Brownson. At any rate, the Cardinal gently suggested, not that I knew nothing at all, but that mastering the catechism would eliminate certain blind spots in my brand of Catholicity, as I had tried to explain it to him.

Perhaps it was something of a jolt to my vanity, but fortunately (or perhaps unfortunately) the Cardinal did not then press the point, and we went on to other things. But I surely took the hint; for in some devious ways I managed, during the following few weeks, to discover and wipe out my blind spots. And after a few more sessions with Monsignor, and certain other priests later on, I found myself safely in God's Strong City.

A rather literal and obtuse non-Catholic, to whom I long afterwards told of this incident and also the Brownson incident, said to me:

"If a person has dipped deeply into theology, as you and Brownson certainly must have done, what in the world could you learn from a simple little penny catechism, such as is used to teach eight- or ten-year-olds? It all sounds very silly to me—like a lot of other Catholic rules and regulations."

"Yes," I replied, "many things sound silly when we know nothing about them. If you realized that there is to be found in the catechism the most fundamental Christian theology that exists, though in brief and simple form, then you *would* know something. You would know that fundamental truth is so simple that it can be grasped even by eight- or ten-year-olds—despite the fact that it is often very confusing to mature but muddled minds. Such is the virtue of Catholic truth."

3.

When once I had been received into the Church, St. Josephs naturally became a "spiritual home" for me, and it was not long before I was familiar with all the phases and activities of the community. That first summer the Cardinal was there practically all the time from late June to September. In July he administered to me the Sacrament of Confirmation in the convent chapel—on Sunday morning. This was quite an inspiring occasion, for many of the Sisters and a goodly number of my family and friends were present. Nobody except my wife and one sponsor had witnessed my reception seven weeks before; no others had seemed interested enough to come—some perhaps doubting that I would go through with it. But now these doubters all flocked in—they saw that it was real.

Throughout that summer many opportunities opened to me for talks with the Cardinal, who was a familiar figure to all the local people for miles around, and was revered by everybody, non-Catholics as well as Catholics. It was his custom on pleasant afternoons, when not tied down by work or callers, to stroll alone through the trails and wooded paths of the spacious St. Josephs grounds. And one thing I early noticed. He seldom failed to go over to the grotto on these afternoon walks, to spend a little time in prayer. There was a long flight of stone steps leading up

to the terrace in front of Our Lady's shrine, which was
visible to passers from the road below. On one occasion,
when driving by in my car, I saw the white head of the
saintly Cardinal just above the bank of shrubs and flowers
which shielded the terrace. He was at his devotions.

And regularly, on his way back to his house on the afternoon walks, he made it a rule to stop at the convent chapel
for a visit to the Blessed Sacrament. Sometimes, when happening to go into the chapel myself, I would see His Eminence kneeling alone in the backmost pew. One Saturday
afternoon when confessions were being heard and the
chapel was half full of children from the camps, the Cardinal came quietly in and kneeled down in the midst of the
children.

"How like him," exclaimed one of his closest New York
friends, to whom I related this incident.

One might devote many pages, did space permit, to enlarge upon the virtues of this truly humble and holy man,
who, by both precept and example, helped me so greatly
to understand the significance of the true Catholic life in
those days when I was so new in the Church. But at least
I cannot refrain from saying a few words regarding one
aspect of his "life of grace," in connection with which I
was greatly helped by him.

4.

One of the many things which the convert of more or
less pagan antecedents may be slow to grasp, is the meaning
and efficacy of prayer—the Catholic meaning. If he has
come out of a Protestant environment, it is likely that to
him "prayer" has been primarily a subjective expression of

the emotions, but little else. And then, later on in life, if religious feeling or emotion has flattened out, and he has long lived as a pagan with no deep religious convictions, the practice as well as the meaning of prayer will have completely passed out of his life. With the loss of religious faith of the emotional type, there seems no longer, of course, any meaning whatever to prayer.

In my own case, even community prayer in church had seemed to demand a state of emotionalism I never could feel in the slightest degree, and merely to say prayers without "feeling" seemed more or less hypocritical. I recollect being present, many years ago, at an old-fashioned Methodist revival meeting—purely out of curiosity, I imagine. The preacher, who was very sensational, exhorted his hearers to pray aloud with "feeling"; to give way to emotion and openly shed tears for their sins. While he was leading his congregation in this intensely emotional way, one of the "deacons" passed up and down the aisle, whispering to the pray-ers to show more emotion, more feeling. Evidently I was cold as ice, for he nudged me and whispered, "Get up steam; get up steam!"

However, in my later years as a nominal Protestant it had long been my custom when attending church services, as I occasionally did, to let the emotional people do all the praying, while I kept consistently silent.

Nowadays a negative attitude towards emotional praying has become more prevalent with many of the sects; you mustn't be too emotional, people are told. In fashionable city churches at least, emotional praying is quite obsolete, except with the older of the faithful. People in this "modern" world seem for the most part to go to church not to pray, but to get inspiration and uplift from music or sermons. And if the music or sermon is not worthwhile, they usually come away without much uplift.

Coming out of that sort of environment, it was quite natural for me to be a little puzzled about prayer; especially liturgical prayer as found in the Catholic Church. This problem of prayer loomed before me in a new way; a startling way at first. Unlike many converts, I had not been frequenting Catholic churches to any great extent before being received; and when I began to study the missal and other Catholic prayer books and read over the various litanies and special forms of devotion, I at first wondered how I could possibly bring myself to "feel," in an emotional way, many things included there. It was all very puzzling.

Now I had of course been drilled in the teaching that the Act of Faith is an act of the intellect and the will, and not of the mere "feelings" or emotions; but it was not at first so apparent to me that the expression of one's faith and devotion through prayer, is also an act of the intellect and will, with the right disposition and intention—even though one may, on occasion, put more or less emotion into the act. One's head should always guide one's heart, not the reverse. It is your intellect and will, formulating your intention, which makes prayer sincere and meaningful; it is not your emotions.

The intelligent Catholic of course knows all this; and that is why he is not troubled or disturbed by occasional aridity or "dryness" in his praying; those times when, while praying with the utmost true intention, he nevertheless does not "feel" like praying.

Correct understanding of prayer and its meaning comes to the convert in time; but perhaps fully as much through example as though precept. And in my own case the example—as well as the teaching—of Cardinal Hayes helped me to understand and to learn how properly to pray, far more than all the books I had read and all the more formal instruction I had received. In various informal talks with him during the summer of 1931 and after, he said much to me about prayer, and particularly emphasized the fact that the Mass itself is always to be understood as the perfect and all inclusive prayer.

Those illuminating talks went far to clarify for me the meaning of the Mass, when I was so new in the Church. I was much confused by the casual statements of some lay Catholics, who told me that while I should not venture to receive Holy Communion without preliminary preparation, this preparation should consist of prayers *not* to be found in the Mass. And I noticed that some Catholics, instead of following the priest in the Mass, spent their time saying their beads before approaching the altar rail. But the Cardinal made it clear to me that the best preparation—the proper preparation—for receiving the Sacrament was to "pray the Mass"; that is, join with the priest all through in offering the great Sacrifice. You perhaps cannot do this in Latin, but you can do it in English. While the Rosary and other devotional prayers are very beneficial, all their efficacy is really drawn from the Sacrifice of Calvary, which is repeatedly offered in every Mass. They are therefore secondary to the Mass itself, and should not replace it. Both preparation for and thanksgiving after the reception of Holy Communion, are found in their perfection in the Mass itself. Any other praying should precede or follow the Mass. Thus, to "pray the Mass" with the priest was my first genuine liturgical lesson—imbibed from the Cardinal.

During my first months in the Church, when trying hard

to follow the priest with an open missal at Mass, I wondered at people around me who were using no missals at all, but just holding their beads. Some didn't seem to be even saying their beads, nor paying much attention to what was going on at the altar. How could these people be said to be really "praying the Mass"? I once asked a missal-less Catholic about this. He glanced at me rather pityingly as he replied, "Well, I've been goin' to Mass near on fifty years. Shouldn't I know it by heart from the first *In nomine Patris* to the last *Deo gratias?*" Of course he should. But did he?

5.

One can readily understand how it came to be that I had such deep devotion and reverence for the saintly Cardinal. But it was not due to these experiences alone. It was not only his counsel and advice, but also his great spiritual personality; his abounding and simple faith; and above all, his deep personal love for and devotion to the poor, the sick and the unfortunate. He was in very truth the "Cardinal of Charities," and, in true imitation of the Good Shepherd, was ever solicitous for the welfare of his flock.

His sudden passing at the close of the summer of 1938 at his St. Josephs home was mourned by the entire countryside. It was less than a week before this sad event that my wife and I spent an hour with him at his house. We were the last lay people outside the community to talk with him at length. We had but recently returned from Europe, having gone there in the late spring to be present at the Eucharistic Congress at Budapest, after which we planned to go down to Rome for a week, where we hoped if possible to have an audience with the Holy Father, Pope Pius XI. This hoped-for audience, which did transpire, and which is described on a later page, had been made possible for us by the kindly aid of Cardinal Hayes himself, and we were naturally eager to tell him something about it.

For most of the summer the Cardinal had been ill and confined to his house. Only once that summer—in early August—had he ventured out to any public function. His last appearance was at the Jubilee celebration of Reverend Mother Polycarpa, that remarkable Superior of the St. Josephs community, whose fifty years as a nun had been filled with good works, all but a few of her earlier years having been spent at St. Josephs. In fact, to all the countryside good Mother Polycarpa *is* St. Josephs—for she has made it what it is.

It was shortly after this Jubilee celebration that the Cardinal sent word for us to call; the last Monday morning in August. We were gratified to find him seemingly well and in good spirits; his voice was strong and his fine blue eyes as bright as ever. But he was obviously quite frail. He talked with us that morning about many things, asking numerous questions about our trip. As usual, he charmed us with his delightful humor; and he had not lost his well known boyish laugh.

As we left him that morning with his blessing, we both were deeply moved. Our last view of him will never be effaced from our memory. He had come out on the porch and stood there as we wended our way down the path to our car. We glanced back from the road below, and there he stood in the doorway, so pale and white and obviously a little tired, but with his bright kindly smile, as he waved us a last good-by, a final God bless you!

The following Saturday night the saintly Cardinal passed

to his reward—in the room above the one where we had talked with him that morning. He had felt fairly strong Saturday afternoon and had gone out for a brief stroll; but after supper he had retired to his room quite early. No one saw him after that. He was at first reported to have died in his sleep; but when his body was discovered the next morning, his reading light was still burning. He had been called to his Divine Master before he had fallen asleep, while no doubt still at his prayers, for his crucifix, when he was found in the morning, was still clasped in his hands.

It is unnecessary to here describe the extraordinary demonstrations of affection for the Cardinal which took place at St. Patrick's Cathedral in New York, where his body lay in state for several days, while vast throngs crowded the Cathedral and blocked the streets to pay their last respects. This has already been told many times. Little has been written, however, of what happened up in the country where the good Cardinal passed away. From the entire countryside, Catholics and non-Catholics alike, crowded into the St. Josephs grounds to pay a last tribute to this Cardinal priest whom they all had loved and admired for so many years. That Sunday afternoon and Monday morning a constant stream of people passed in and out of the house. Many of these people may never have known him well enough to speak with him, but they all held him in deep affection. And that is why they came to make this last gesture of devotion to the revered Cardinal of Charities, who had resided among them for so many years.

CHAPTER FIVE

EARLY GLIMPSES OF THE CATHOLIC SCENE

I.

TO LENGTHEN OR BROADEN one's view or perspective is usually the result of one's own personal experiences. This is especially so in the case of the convert who is beginning to get a vision of his new religious home from the inside. The view he had of the Church from the outside was necessarily but a partial view; and in most cases a view which had been distorted by long years of erroneous fancies and myopic conceptions.

That surely, was the case with me. Never, until I began to see the Catholic Church from the inside, had I any full realization of her wholly unique status among the institutions of mankind. Not until actually a member did I begin to consciously reflect on the fact that in becoming a Catholic I had become a unit of not only the oldest, but by far the largest, most vital and most far-flung institution on the face of the globe.

It is undoubtedly true with many a convert (even if fairly well versed in the facts of history) that the world-wide extent and great age of the Church are not very consciously realized at first. It may be that he has read much religious and secular history, and is already vaguely familiar with the fact that the Catholic Church "was great and respected before the Saxon set foot on Britain, before the

Frank had crossed the Rhine, when Grecian eloquence still
flourished in Antioch, when idols were still worshipped
in the temple of Mecca" (to quote Lord Macaulay), but
even so it will probably take him some time to orient himself as one of the units of this vast, age-old organism.

In time, however, as he grows familiar with the external
and internal workings of the Church, studies her liturgy
and its development from ancient times, becomes more familiar with her history throughout the centuries, and grasps
the full significance of her sacramental system and the why
and wherefore of her discipline—the unity and solidarity
of the Church will become increasingly understood. And
very soon one tremendous fact will stand out, the fact that
the Catholic Church possesses four distinct marks which
distinguish her from every other Christian body in this
world. Alone of all the "Christianities," she is One; she is
Holy; she is Catholic; and she is Apostolic. Although some
other Christian groups may sometimes have displayed characteristics of holiness, yet none of them are truly catholic
(that is to say, universal); none are directly Apostolic in
their genesis or authority, and certainly none of them display "one-ness" in the sense of unity and solidarity, either
in their teachings of faith and morals, or in organization
and structure.

Now in the experience of the average newcomer, the full
realization of the unity and solidarity of the Church, as well
as her unique universality, will probably sink into his consciousness fully as much through his personal experiences
in his new home, as through study or any other process of
research. Well do I recall reading as a youth, the half dozen
volumes of Hallam's *Middle Ages*, which of course, in
covering the Ages of Faith, contains many references to

the Catholic Church. Nearly every chapter brings in some activities of the Church. No history of those ages, secular or other, could possibly avoid the inclusion of much Catholic history, for in those days Christianity and Catholicism were interchangeable terms. And yet the fact of her catholicity never particularly impressed me. Later in life I read many other histories of the Christian centuries and twice struggled through the ten volumes of Gibbon's *Rome;* and yet I never visualized this Catholic Church of the ages in her true setting until after I had become a member. Only when actually in the Church did all this take on reality for me.

Probably those who move about within their native land or beyond its borders, more easily acquire a broadening vision of the Church's universal characteristics than do those who always stay at home. For not only in his own home town or within his own country, but thousands of miles from home, in Europe, Asia, Africa, South America, Australasia and in the islands of the seven seas, the open doors of Catholic churches and cathedrals, with the tabernacle upon the altar and the familiar sanctuary light, give the visiting Catholic a "homey" feeling, such as he could not possibly experience if not a Catholic.

It is not merely within his own neighborhood, or within the borders of his native land, that the Catholic can go to Mass and join with the priest in offering up the eternal Sacrifice of Calvary. He can do this freely—at least in peace times—in London, Paris, Rome, Vienna, Budapest, Athens, Tokio, Singapore, Manila, Buenos Aires or Cape Town; in fact, almost anywhere in the world and, for this brief hour at least, be as completely "at home" as he would be in his own parish church. When in foreign lands he may not know one word of the local language spoken, may find it impossible to move about without a guide; but he is familiar with the Latin Mass, and can join in it and receive Holy Communion precisely as he would do in his own home town.

This fact of being able to go to Mass wherever the Catholic happens to be, profoundly impressed me even before my own Catholic days. For instance, happening to be in the city of Algiers for a few brief hours a dozen years ago, and starting out to get a glimpse of the city and of one or two famous Arab mosques, I noticed a large group of white-clad nuns passing down the street. Assuming that they were not Christians but Mohammedan Sisters of some sort, I was interested enough to stop and watch them. Shortly they turned a corner and entered a doorway on a side street. The building did not look like a mosque, but curiosity inspired me to peek in. I found it was a Catholic Church. Mass was just beginning; a priest was ascending the altar steps. Not then being a Catholic I felt like an intruder. But any Catholic, from America or any part of the world, would have been utterly at home there.

Naturally it is only the occasional convert who has opportunities to see Catholicity functioning in foreign lands; but anyone can get plenty of experience of this kind within his own country if he moves about a bit. And if he is observant he will have many surprises. He will not only be surprised at the extent of living Catholicity he will find in unexpected places, but perhaps he will also be surprised that the limited notions regarding Catholicism he himself held before he became a Catholic, are really quite universal among non-Catholics. That is, ignorance of Catholic vitality on the part of most non-Catholics in any city or town he visits, will probably surprise him—even though he may have been equally unobservant in his own non-Catholic days.

Let me cite an instance of this. Incidents, humorous or other, often help one to envisage the Catholic scene more effectively than mere description or explanation. Moreover, in the recital of incidents truth is often driven home more effectively than through long-drawn-out dissertations. That is one reason why the pages of this book are dotted with the portrayal of incidents of one kind or another.

Shortly after my own Catholic life began, having occasion late in the month of May to stop over on business at Lafayette, Indiana, I was driven down from Chicago by a good Protestant friend. It was the eve of Ascension Thursday. Remarking to my driver friend on the way, that I must go to Mass somewhere in Lafayette the next morning, he surprised me by very positively stating, "You won't be able to do that in Lafayette. I know this section of Indiana well and I can tell you it's solidly Protestant. I doubt if you will find any Catholic church nearer than Indianapolis."

But after reaching Lafayette that afternoon and asking the hotel clerk if there was a Catholic church in town, he immediately directed me to three. However, he was himself so ignorant of what was going on Catholic-wise in his own city, that he expressed great surprise when I said I expected to go to the nearest Catholic church before breakfast the next morning. He was sure *all* the churches in Lafayette were open Sundays only!

The next morning at seven o'clock it was with the exultant pride of the new convert that I was able to show my Protestant friend (who accompanied me) the inside of a

Catholic church on Ascension Thursday. The church was one of the largest in Lafayette—St. Boniface—and was of course crowded to the doors, all seats occupied and many standing in the rear. It was but one of five or six Masses that day. No doubt this was quite unsuspected by many of the still sleeping non-Catholics of the city. But anyhow, I had given my Protestant friend a glimpse of the vitality of the Church in a place where he had assured me there were no Catholics.

An equally instructive—and more amusing—incident still sticks in my memory. This time it was Chicago; perhaps a year after the Lafayette incident.

The day after my arrival on this particular visit was a First Friday. Having a busy day in prospect for that Friday, I decided to arise early and go to Mass at six at the Holy Name Cathedral, which was but a short distance from my hotel. On awaking at 5:30 it was raining hard, and as it was late November, still dark as midnight. I had no umbrella and wondered if I could get a taxi at that early hour. As luck would have it one lone taxi stood at the corner, the driver fast asleep.

It was a dubious-looking affair; an old "sea-going" wreck. The driver was snoring, but on my tapping on the window he awoke, rubbed a pair of bleary eyes, pulled himself together, reached over to open the side door in the usual way, and I stepped in. But before I could say a word or was even seated, we were tearing down the street. In a flash I thought of kidnappers. "Hold on," I yelled, "where are you taking me?"

"*Holy Name Cathedral!*" he shouted back. And wonderingly I settled back in the seat. We arrived within a few minutes, after two or three hair breadth escapes from near-collisions. As I paid the fare I asked this miraculous mind reader:

"How did you know I wanted to come here?"

Glancing around at the crowds who even at that early hour were flocking into the cathedral in the pouring rain, and winking one of his bloodshot eyes, he said:

"Fer what else would a guy be goin' out sober this early on a wet mornin'? I knew ye were Catlick. Ye sure have the look!"

The cathedral was crowded, of course. And with the continuing exultant pride of the new convert—that shown at Lafayette not yet having worn away!—when I got back to the hotel to meet three business men who were to break-fast with me, I did not fail to speak of the great crowd at the cathedral at six o'clock in the morning. These men were not Catholics, and one of them asked:

"Was it a convention or something?"

2.

Did space permit I could recount many other incidents of this general character which throw much light on the human side of the Catholic scene. And perhaps throughout later chapters some will be elaborated on. But while, in traveling in America, an interesting panorama is certain to unfold for the Catholic novice, it is really when he goes abroad that his realization of the universal scope of the Church comes more definitely to the surface.

It was so with me. For many years I had been interested in European history and particularly in the history of Great Britain, and I had recently been reading much regarding the persecution in England of Catholics, from the days of

Henry VIII and throughout the reign of Queen Elizabeth, so a desire to go there and see something of British Catholicism as it is nowadays, came bubbling to the surface early in my new Catholic life.

At that particular time—1931—the activities of English Catholics were getting much publicity in America. One read about them in the Catholic papers all the time. Moreover, much of my own reading of Catholic literature during the previous few years had centered on British writers —Chesterton, Belloc, Fathers Knox and Martindale, not to mention Cardinal Newman and other writers of his and later days. And there seemed to be at that time a veritable stream of notable British conversions to the Faith. It was therefore natural for me to be eager to see, with my own eyes, the modern Catholic side of England—especially in London, that old stronghold of Protestantism. I already knew London well, having been there many times in the course of thirty years, and I still had important business interests there. But all earlier visits had occurred before my Catholic days, when any interest I may have had in religion, was purely nominal.

The winter and spring of 1932 was a busy, hectic time for me at home; American finances were beginning to collapse, banks were failing by the score all across the country; the outlook was dire indeed; but despite it all I managed to squeeze out a few weeks for a short trip to London and Paris, hoping to get at least a brief glimpse of Catholicism there, and if possible meet a few native Catholics. Up to that time I knew not a single Catholic outside the United States.

My wife and I sailed the day after Easter on the old *Mauretania*. It was a pleasant journey; a smooth sea and a small passenger list. There happened to be three American priests on board bound for Rome, and convert-like, I saw to it that they met me on the first day out. The new convert never misses a chance on his travels to let other Catholics (especially priests) know that he is one of them. It is later on that he gets over all that.

I had once before, on a short visit to London in 1928, slipped into the beautiful monument of the resurrection of Catholicism in London—Westminster Cathedral—but not then having progressed very far in my pilgrimage to the Catholic Church, that visit had made but a superficial impression. But this time the situation was of quite another kind. The first thing I did after registering at the hotel and unpacking, was to hop into a cab and hurry over to the Cathedral that Sunday afternoon, in the hope of arriving in time for Vespers or Compline, or at least for Benediction. I was just in time for the latter; and then I lingered on for a couple of hours, for now this monument of the Faith was full of new meaning for me.

I recollect meditating for long that afternoon in this great basilica, on the epochal revival of the Catholic Church in the England of the nineteenth century. How well did this majestic edifice, still so new and incomplete, yet so full of meaning, typify the revival and extension of the ancient Faith in this land of its long persecution. Here it stood in the heart of Protestant London, at no great distance from the much older Westminster Abbey, which had been the great center of Catholicity prior to the devastation wrought by the politicians, schismatics and heretics of the sixteenth and seventeenth centuries. The beautiful old abbey, it seemed to me, had become less a church than a secular hall of fame, being cluttered up with the monuments and memorials of British politicians, statesmen, soldiers and sailors, royalty and literati of every sort, regardless of their Christian or non-Christian beliefs. The earlier memorials of saints and great churchmen had long been overshadowed by all this.

But the newer Westminster Cathedral, in its loveliness and its atmosphere of sanctity, brought to mind the long past centuries of true Catholic culture; it restored to mind and memory those ages of faith, those days when England was proud to be known as Mary's Dower; it made live again the times of St. Anselm, St. Dunstan, St. Edmund, St. Thomas of Canterbury, and so many other Catholic champions who worked and wrought for the Church of Christ.

And the Church's "second spring," as Newman so aptly called it, came vividly to mind under the roof of this great cathedral. One was inspired to recall those reviving days of the nineteenth century, from the times of the great Bishop Milner, and on down through the years in a steadily widening and deepening stream, with Cardinals Wiseman, Manning, Newman, Vaughan and Bourne; with the great Bishop Ullathorne, Fathers Faber and Spencer, William George Ward, and numerous other outstanding leaders and converts to the Faith. Particularly was one inspired in this atmosphere to reflect anew on the great convert movement to the Church during and after the conversion and subsequent work of Newman, when more than a thousand of the Anglican clergy followed in his footsteps—and are still following.

3.

There now followed for me a busy and exciting fortnight, during which I was privileged to meet numerous interesting personalities in London Catholic circles. My good friend Michael Williams of the New York *Commonweal* had supplied me with a sheaf of letters of introduction to many whom he knew I would like to meet. An utter stranger among British Catholics, I would have been helpless without them. But they were an open sesame, as soon became apparent; for nearly all I met were only too glad to put me in touch with others.

Being young and vigorous in those days—as I still am, I hope!—it did not exhaust me to rush around. I kept going morning, noon and night. Among those whom I now met for the first time was the late Father Francis Woodlock, brother of Thomas F. Woodlock of the *Wall Street Journal*, one of my oldest friends in the financial world. Father Woodlock was delightful, and made me feel thoroughly at home at Farm Street. It was through him that I was able to meet the well-known Father Martindale, the author of so many fine Catholic books. I found Father Martindale perched at his typewriter in his study, where he carried on a long conversation with me while banging away on a manuscript which apparently had to be completed that day. As he tore finished sheets from his machine he would drop them to the floor, and the tops of his windows being down in the customary English fashion, the wind kept these sheets of copy flying about the room. A veritable live wire was Father Martindale. It seemed to me that he had anything but a one track mind; it was ten track; for he talked on several subjects concurrently and never seemed to lose himself for a moment; and continued to bang away on his typewriter all the while. Evidently that is why his literary production has been so prolific.

Then there was Father Martin D'Arcy, S.J., whose

latest book, *The Nature of Belief*, I had been trying to absorb while coming over on the steamer. I had found it much easier to digest than Cardinal Newman's well-known book on the same subject—his *Grammar of Assent*. It had required three close readings before I had digested that. I was glad to tell Father D'Arcy that his book seemed much more lucid to my simple mind.

Mention should not be omitted of the visit to the Farm Street church the following Sunday, where Father D'Arcy preached one of the finest sermons I have ever heard. To see this London church thronged, just as would be the great Jesuit church in New York—St. Ignatius Loyola—gave me a slight hint of the vitality of Catholicism in old London town.

Far less of a strain on my untrained mind than had been my attempted discussion of theological matters with Fathers Martindale and D'Arcy, was a delightful visit with Gilbert K. Chesterton. He was at that time hard at work on his brilliant short life of St. Thomas Aquinas, which was published the following year; and he told me, with much humor, of his struggles to picture St. Thomas as a real human being, and not as a mere philosopher.

That was indeed one of the high spots of our London stay. My wife and I were invited for tea at the Chesterton London home opposite Westminster Cathedral, so we were privileged to meet the delightful Mrs. Chesterton also.

Long had I been hoping for an opportunity to meet G. K. Chesterton. His great book, *Orthodoxy*, had been of far-reaching influence in my own conversion, and later on I had read and digested nearly all his serious writings. His splendid book of later years, *The Everlasting Man*, had long been one of my favorites; indeed, my wife had always held

that this book had done more to make me a Catholic than
the earlier one—and you may be sure she passed this opinion on to "G. K." I did not gainsay her, for perhaps she was
right, or nearly so. If it was *Orthodoxy* that first started me
on the road to straight thinking regarding the deeper things
of life, certainly the later book had carried on the good
work, for I recollect having gone back to it again and again
during the unraveling of many perplexities.

At any rate, it was a real privilege to talk with this distinguished man, and I surely did learn a great deal from
him, even in this short conversation of an hour or two.

Perhaps the most gratifying experience of all was in
meeting the late Cardinal Bourne with whom, through the
kindness of Frank J. Sheed, I was enabled to talk on two
occasions; first at a big reception given that week by the
Cardinal to all the British hierarchy and numerous of the
laity; and also some days later at a delightful private audience. The Cardinal was charming and profoundly impressed me with his fine personality, his deep Catholicity.
He gave me a most interesting outline of the state of the
Church in Great Britain, and of his high hopes for her future
there.

Before that fortnight was over I had met a host of interesting people, both clerical and lay, and began to feel quite
at home in London Catholic circles. My knowledge was
being greatly expanded by visiting many of London's Catholic churches and religious houses, few of which I had ever
seen before. How well I recall getting soaked to the skin
on a rainy morning while searching in the neighborhood of
High Holborn for the famous old St. Etheldreda's church,
and being steered by a stupid passer-by to a Wesleyan
chapel in the neighborhood! When I finally did locate St.

Etheldreda's, water oozed from my shoes as I walked up the aisle. And it is with amusement I recollect a visit to Brompton Oratory, where I went to confession and the priest in the box startled me by saying, "You seem new at it. You must be a convert!"

4.

Mention of Brompton Oratory quite naturally recalls to mind the so-called Oxford Movement of a century ago in the Church of England—as anything relating to Newman does. And right here may be the best place to tell of one of those incidents which often happen to converts from the Church of England, or from the Protestant Episcopal Church in the United States.

Americans whose affiliations are with Protestant bodies like the Presbyterian, Baptist, Lutheran or Methodist, are apt to know little and care less about the so-called Oxford Movement in the Anglican Church. But with the convert from the Protestant Episcopal Church this is less true. For the Oxford Movement was a "catholic" movement. It was an attempt, on the part of a group of Anglican clergy (the leaders being mostly Oxford men) to revive in the Anglican Church the orthodoxy which had been largely characteristic during the days of King Charles I, under Archbishop Laud and his school. That early High Church movement had not lasted. The Puritans and Covenanters got in the saddle and beheaded both the Archbishop and the King. And while there were attempts at revival of this movement after the Restoration in the time of Charles II, by the early years of the eighteenth century the Church had again lapsed far from orthodoxy. What came to be known as Latitudinarianism spread through the Establishment—a general attitude towards traditional dogma which we would nowadays call Modernism. This was later tempered somewhat by the rise of Evangelicalism, more orthodox in some respects, but in no sense a movement toward Catholic beliefs. It was just old-fashioned emotional Protestantism.

As a result of this drifting away from orthodox Christianity, with rejection of all real belief in revealed truth, the Anglican Establishment had, by the early nineteenth century, so seriously declined in its spiritual status that many despaired of its life. Finally there arose, towards the end of the 1820's, much open agitation in favor of a merger with the more vital Non-conformist sects—the Calvinistic communions—just as today we are witnessing an attempt, by a section of the American Protestant Episcopal Church, to bring about a merger with the Presbyterians. Indeed, it was then admitted by various Anglican divines, among whom was the eminent Dr. Thomas Arnold, that if a merger of all the Protestant bodies in England did not soon take place, the Establishment (State-controlled Anglican Church) would dry up and disappear.

It was just at this time that a group of young Anglican clergy, most of them Oxford men led by John Keble, John Henry Newman and Edwin B. Pusey, began to issue their "Tracts for the Times," a series of essays, all quite Catholic in tone; the purpose being to awaken in the Anglican Church a consciousness of the old orthodox beliefs. These activities, persisted in over a series of years, gained widespread support, but also caused heated discussion and powerful opposition. A great rift was started in the Anglican communion which persists to this day. A large majority of both the clergy and laity, in both the Anglican Church and the Protestant Episcopal Church in America, have continued to be "latitudinarian," some moderately and some aggressively so. But an active aggressive minority have adhered to the teachings of the Oxford revival, many going even farther in a Catholic direction. The latter are the "Anglo-Catholics" of today.

Familiar enough to English people of all faiths, and to most Protestant Episcopalians in America, these facts are obscure to the average Roman Catholic—who is apt to be puzzled when he hears some Protestant Episcopalian calling himself a "Catholic." But in view of my own background I was not at all puzzled when, just at the time of this London visit, I received from an "Anglo-Catholic" friend a cordial letter of welcome into the Catholic Church. "Now that you are *one of us*," he said, "let us both pray for the day when we shall see the Pope pontificate in St. Peter's with the Archbishop of Canterbury and the Patriarch of Constantinople as his deacons."

A kindly wish, which I understood better than would the average American Catholic. The latter would be likely to assume that my friend had asked me to pray for the day when the Archbishop of Canterbury and the Patriarch of Constantinople would see the error of their ways and return to the Catholic Church. But he would be wildly wrong in this assumption, for my "Anglo-Catholic" friend believes that the Archbishop and the Patriarch are already in the Catholic Church. He believes in what is called the branch theory; a theory first talked of in the days of Henry VIII, but never seriously promoted until the days of Dr. Pusey; and never accepted officially by any of the so-called "branches."

What is this theory? It is the contention that the visible Church on earth founded by Christ has failed in her unity; that the Holy Spirit, Who guards Christ's Church from error in teaching faith and morals, now guides three churches, all three contradicting one another in fundamental teachings. The three churches, so guided, according to this branch theory, are the Anglican Church (High, Low, Broad or Modernist); the Orthodox Churches of the East (in sixteen or eighteen divisions); and the Roman Catholic Church. I say it in all reverence, but it seems to me that the Holy Spirit is having terrific demands put upon Him, for in addition to all this, a multitude of Protestant sects of diverse teachings claim His guidance also!

This branch theory, together with the claim that Anglican bishops possess genuine Apostolic Orders, constitutes the cornerstone of the "Anglo-Catholic" division in the Church of England and the similar division in the Protestant Episcopal Church in America.

Of course I wouldn't think of starting any argument with my good "Anglo-Catholic" friend. He was in good faith, sincerely believing in the soundness of his position; and anyhow he already knew my own view in this matter. Perhaps I might have suggested that he read Father Woodlock's little book, *Constantinople, Canterbury and Rome*,[1] that illuminating review of Bishop Gore's theory of the Catholic Church. If one reads that little book (as I did before I became a Catholic) one begins to wonder why the so-called branch theory is invoked even by an "Anglo-Catholic." Or if I had wanted to get into a more serious controversy I might have suggested that he read Pope Leo XIII's encyclical on Anglican Orders. But who knows

[1] *Constantinople, Canterbury and Rome*, by Rev. Francis Woodlock, S.J., Longmans, Green & Co., London, 1925.

better than I do that mere disputation seldom accomplishes anything? Nobody ever changed my beliefs by that method! He was a shrewd judge of human nature who said that the man convinced against his will is of the same opinion still.

*　　*　　*

That brief visit to London did much to broaden my vision of the general Catholic scene. We also spent ten days in Paris that spring, which enabled me to get a slight glimpse of the Church there. I found Catholicism in Paris far more alive than I had supposed it to be. The modern French Catholic revival was even then well under way. I shall not, however, burden my readers further with foreign experiences in this chapter; there will be references to the foreign field on later pages.

CHAPTER SIX

AT LEAST YOU CAN SHOW THEM

1.

CRADLE CATHOLICS MAY OFTEN view converts as queer people, especially during their early years of conversion mania; that period when we newcomers assume that every inquirer about Catholic doctrines or customs is a ripe prospect for easy conversion. But converts often feel that the cradle Catholics are the queer ones. They are, for instance, sceptics, cynics, when we joyfully announce to them that Bill Jones, who has all his life been a hater of the Church, is now under instruction and will shortly be received. Usually they won't believe there is anything in it until it has become a fact. And when it does become a fact, they probably shrug their shoulders and say, "Why get excited about a little thing like that? He probably won't stick, anyway."

But you know, these converts usually do stick. In nearly all cases they stick. And it is because converts so uniformly stick that other converts take them seriously; far more seriously than do the cradle Catholics. It is no doubt very largely a case of fellow-feeling. Most convert-Catholics continue convert-conscious all their lives long. Despite many tragic disappointments, they always cherish an undying hope that various Toms, Dicks and Harrys whom they know, will sooner or later see the light and come into the Church. And when this does occasionally happen, their joy is unconfined—as every convert-Catholic knows.

Of course all converts are frequently fooled—particularly during their early Catholic years. I was often quite ludicrously fooled. Whether it was because I am too much of an optimist or too poor a judge of men, I cannot say. Anyhow, it took me a long time to get over the notion that anyone who asked me a leading question about the Church, was necessarily a promising prospect for conversion.

The ordinary cradle Catholic, whenever approached by an inquiring outsider, will be almost certain to say, "I'm not qualified to explain the Catholic religion; go and talk with a priest." But not so the convert—unless his wisdom teeth are cut. Little as he is qualified to do so, he will start right in and try to instruct the inquirer on the spot. That's why he suffers so many disappointments. He thinks he sees a live prospect; he shoots—and hits a dud.

Take my own case. Someone would say to me, "I hear you have become a Catholic. How interesting! Do tell me all about it." And I would joyfully reflect—ah, here's a fine opening for conversion work. Then I would probably start a tiresome discussion of Catholic doctrines and dogmas, quite oblivious of the fact that after the first quarter hour, my listener, being bored, was no longer following me. He might show some polite attention; perhaps give me some sympathetic nods; but the more nods I got the more I would keep on talking. Then I would probably wind up by offering to send him some book, and perhaps he would politely thank me for that. For days or weeks thereafter I would be happily reflecting that he must be getting a lot out of the book and would soon seek me out for another interview—not realizing that the book, which had cost me two dollars, was still in its wrapper unopened.

Or some friend might say, "I've got no religion myself, but I've always thought that if I did get one, it would be the Catholic religion." That statement gives you a thrill. You at once offer to help him get the Catholic religion, and immediately begin to lead him on. He may patiently listen until the point of exhaustion is reached; but the next time you meet him he is careful to steer all conversation into channels which have no connection with religion.

Then there are those occasions when someone says to you: "Poor old Smith is at loose ends. What he needs is a religion. Perhaps the Catholic religion would be just the thing for him. Why don't you follow him up?" And on the strength of this hint you get busy at once. You first invite Smith to luncheon or dinner. Gladly he accepts and consumes your food with gusto while you try to lead him into the Church. You may think you have made an impression; but after that not even the temptation to enjoy more of your delectable food will draw Smith nigh. He now makes it his business to keep far away from you.

There are also those instances where people ask you, for some absurd or trivial reason, to help them get into the Church. I recall one of these instances; it involved a callow youth in his twenties, who approached me one day in my first Catholic year. He wanted me to tell him "the easiest, quickest and cheapest way" to become a Catholic. After a short talk I found that he was not in the least interested in knowing anything about the Catholic religion; he was only interested in a young Catholic girl whom he wished to marry. She had refused him, he said, because he was not a Catholic. On the chance that this circumstance might lead to something real, I gave him a card to a priest with whom, I suggested, he might discuss the matter. Of course he never went near the priest. And that was the end of that.

Nevertheless, despite such experiences, I continued for a long time to cherish the notion that most serious inquirers were ripe prospects for easy conversion, and that no opportunity should be overlooked for toppling them into the basket. I had to suffer a long line of disappointments before being cured. Some say I am not cured yet; and that may be so, for I still do allow myself to be fooled now and then—on the chance of accidentally hitting the bullseye. . . .

2.

Perhaps because of this persistently optimistic attitude, a few years ago I was quite amusingly misled by allowing a certain old friend to loom up before me as a particularly hot prospect. I had long regarded him as the merest romanticist in matters of religion; one of the pantheistic sort who revel in poetical fancies of one sort or another without ever getting down to anything objective. Although he had shown sympathetic interest on my becoming a Catholic several years before, I had never thought of him at all as a potential convert until he said to me one evening at a social gathering:

"For a long time I've been wanting to have a serious talk with you about the Catholic Church. You seem to have found something real; I must admit that I envy you. I do wish that I might feel as happy and serene about my own religion; but I am anything but satisfied. Can't we have a talk about your beliefs?"

What an opportunity! Here was an opening not to be ignored. Here was the ideal situation for promising missionary work. At once I suggested that he have luncheon with me so we might discuss the subject at length. He accepted with alacrity and we met a few days later. I was all primed to lead him right into the Catholic Church.

In opening our discussion I first asked him how much of the Christian religion he already believed, or did he believe any of it?

"Oh yes, I'm a Christian of course," he replied with great emphasis. "What I suppose you would call a *liberal* Christian. I'll admit I've never taken much interest in creeds and such things; but I do like uplifting sermons and a certain amount of ritual in church—when properly done. Indeed, I am a Christian."

"Well, if you are *really* a Christian, then we may not be so far apart, after all. Anyone who believes in the existence of God and the divinity of Christ is already at least halfway to the Catholic Church. All you need do is to logically follow and accept the consequences of those basic beliefs. If you do that without prejudice and with an open mind, and are honest with yourself, you are certain to finally land at the door of the Catholic Church."

His reaction to all that was a puzzled stare. Then, after a lapse of some minutes, knitting his brow, he said:

"But perhaps my idea of God is different from the Catholic idea. You Catholics say you believe in a 'personal' God. Now that's not my idea of God at all."

"What is your idea?" I asked.

"Why, to me God is—well—everything—everywhere—universal. God is nature, beauty, truth, love, inspiration; in fact a mysterious *something* which baffles precise definition. Some define it as the divine spark of the universe; and perhaps that's as good a definition as any."

"I thought so," I laughed. "Pantheism—theosophy. You believe in a sort of kaleidoscopic god. You see your god through a kaleidoscope, and as you turn it around you see something different in every turning. No wonder you are dissatisfied with your religion. It reminds me of the story of the preacher who once asked his flock from the pulpit to explain to him their idea of God. One of his parishioners arose and replied that his idea was that somewhere up in the sky there is a big oblong blur, and that blur is God. The preacher then asked him if he loved God, to which question he replied affirmatively. 'Well,' remarked the preacher, 'that is a most wonderful sort of love—to love a big oblong blur.'

"And by the same token I ask you, my friend, how you bring yourself to love your kaleidoscopic god? You say, for instance, that your idea of God is 'a mysterious something which baffles definition'! How in heaven's name, can anyone love—really love—a mysterious something which baffles definition?"

Once more my prospect indulged in his puzzled stare. Then he looked intently at the vacant face of the big fat waiter, who was leaning over our table clearing away the crumbs. Finally, when the waiter turned away, he said:

"Perhaps I didn't make myself clear. What I mean is we find God in nature—don't we? I can't see the point of a 'personal' God. I see God as beauty, as harmony, as the birds and flowers, just as St. Francis of Assisi did—didn't he?"

"As St. Francis *did not*. He saw the evidences and reflections of God's love in the nature which He had created

—as we all do, of course. He would see the proof of God's reality in the fact that you, with your immortal soul, are alive right now. But he would never see you *as* God, or as a part of God."

"Of course not. But I don't claim to be a part of God. Where did you get that idea?"

"Why, you just told me that you view nature and God as one and the same. And certainly, as you have a human, natural body, you are a part of nature. That makes you 'a part of God,' doesn't it?"

A vacant stare, then "Hmm! I never thought of it in that way. It's nonsense, of course. But, how do you explain the existence of nature, if God and nature are not the same?"

"That's the question I was waiting for you to ask," I replied. "The existence of nature is explained in only one way. Nature was created by God, the creator of us all."

Knitting his brow once more my companion said with great seriousness: "Do you know I could never believe that. This Bible story about God creating everything by mere mandate, never was convincing to me, not even as a youth; and when I learned about Darwin with his idea of evolution, I saw that I was right. Nature evolved; it wasn't created at all."

"Then your idea is that God 'evolved' also, for you hold that God and nature are one and the same thing."

"Well—yes, in a way, I suppose."

"Then tell me; what did nature—God—evolve from? What existed before this evolution began? How could nature start evolving if nothing theretofore existed?"

Another puzzled stare; another deep knit in the brow. Again he studied the vacant face of the big fat waiter, and finally ventured to say, "I'll be damned if I know. What is your idea?"

"There's only one possible answer," I said. "In only one way could life begin; and that is, through *creation*. You cannot explain anything in the universe unless you start with the postulate of an eternally existing, omnipotent, transcendent creator; that is to say, with the eternal existence of God. You talk about evolution. But that is not fundamental. The fundamental problem is not how this universe or cosmos functions or develops; it is not a question of the processes of nature, *but how things began; how they came to be*. And also, *why* things are as they are; why nature, why we human beings, as well as all life around us, exist and function at all. We men cannot at all understand ourselves unless we know what we are here for—the purpose of our creation and existence. We may be able to explain physical and psychological traits in ourselves; we may be able to unravel a lot of the apparent mysteries of our makeup, but unless we know *why* we are here on this earth we really know nothing at all."

Obviously my listener was floundering in his efforts to follow the argument, for he now said:

"What you say sounds reasonable to me, though I never thought of it in that way before. You must be right; there must have been creation to start with. But still I can't see why God and nature—God and the cosmos—are not one and the same thing."

"Ah! Then you agree that the universe must have been created? But who created it?"

"God must have created it."

"You are right; He did. But you insist that God and the universe are one and the same thing. So, according to your idea God must have created God. Is that what you think?"

His mascot, the big fat waiter, now got another long stare, as my knitted brow listener hesitatingly ventured,

"Well, why not? . . . If God could create the universe, why could He not create—create—Himself? What?"

That, I thought, was the climax; it was a hopeless case. Actually, educated and cultured as this person was supposed to be, he could reason no better than that. He could not see the absurdity of believing that a non-existent being —nothing—could create an existent Being—God.

This inability to do even elementary reasoning is often characteristic of college-bred men, who, while they may have absorbed a mountain of rhetoric, have never been taught to think. Often we find men of no education whatever, able to reason far more logically than some who possess university diplomas. This fact was proven on the spot that day. My prospect was called to the telephone, and while he was gone, the big fat waiter, who had been hovering around and listening in, ventured to make a remark. Said he, "If you will excuse me, sir, the gentleman seems a bit off his eggs. Nothin' can't be made out o' nothin', 'cept by God A'mighty. If there wasn't *always* God A'mighty, how in hell could *anything* begin to be?"

My prospect missed that wisp of wisdom. When he returned he had evidently lost the thread of the argument. "Well, it's all very interesting," he resumed. "But still I don't get your Catholic idea of God. What I call God is something mysterious in nature which appeals to the emotions but baffles exact definition—as I said before. Now let us take up the other matter—the divinity of Christ."

"What's the use of going into that?" I asked. "If you don't believe in the existence of a 'personal' God as an eternal Being, it isn't possible to believe in the divinity of Christ."

"But I *do* believe in the divinity of Christ. Not in the Catholic sense, perhaps. What I believe is that He was divine as all men are divine who have the spirit of God in their hearts; and I believe He was the Son of God in the same sense that all men are sons of God. That is the modern common-sense view, isn't it?"

"I should call it the modern nonsensical view to term that the 'divinity of Christ.' If Jesus Christ was not God Incarnate, then Christianity is a mere delusion, a fantasy. The Catholic has no sympathy with the modern efforts to strip Christ of His divinity, and to twist His plain words by reading new meanings into them. His Apostles—after His Resurrection—understood what He meant when He spoke —and no man spoke as this Man spoke—and it is what they understood that the Catholic Church teaches today and has always taught."

"But isn't it true that modern research has given us a different explanation of all that? Now, men like Bertrand Russell——"

"Ah ha! You mention Bertrand Russell—not a Christian at all. That's like asking the Shah of Persia to interpret the American Constitution, isn't it? Anyhow, why assume that non-believers who are living nineteen centuries after the event, know the mind of Christ better than those who saw Him daily and spoke with Him? The witness of Matthew, Mark, Luke, Peter, Paul, James and John and the Fathers immediately following them, is what the Catholic Church points to; not to the witness of any group of sceptics who live nineteen centuries later."

"Well," said my prospect, as he glanced at his watch, "you seem to be repeating things about Christ which I was taught in a Protestant Sunday school, but later dropped as childish. I thought the Catholic Church was more *progressive* than that. I expected to hear something *new*. Hasn't the Catholic Church some up-to-date ideas?"

Alas, my hot prospect was nothing but a dud. I promised at parting to send him a couple of books on Catholic teachings, which he said he would be glad to read. I hoped they might at least start him on a little straight thinking. However, my optimism was too great; for that was the end, insofar as his interest in Catholicism was concerned. More than a year passed before I had any chance to talk with him again. When we finally did meet he was obviously not interested in knowing any more about my religion, but I ventured to ask him if he had gotten anything out of the two books I had sent him the year before. He simply raised his eyebrows in puzzled surprise and stared. And then, with that habitual wrinkling of his brow he asked, "What books?"

Discouraging, wasn't it? All that effort for nothing. But that is a mere sample of what is coming to the convert who naïvely thinks that pantheistically inclined minds who make casual inquiries about the Catholic Faith, are ripe prospects for easy conversion. I could recount other incidents of the same type. The woods are full of these muddle-minded people. No doubt most of them are sincere and in good faith; but they are of the type of "hot" prospect who seldom become Catholics, despite any nostalgia they may have for the Church. They continue to revel in their wilderness of words until they pass into eternity.

3.

Yet there is a brighter side to this conversion business also. For there are many opportunities where one may influence a conversion without starting any arguments, explaining or defending any dogmas, or donating any books. One such case of an outstanding nature I do know, and while I had nothing to do with it myself, it makes an interesting little story, besides pointing a moral to all would-be Catholic missionaries like you and me.

One evening seven or eight years ago, an agnostic who could easily have been classed as a hard nut to crack—for he was intolerant towards all religion—happened to meet, in a hotel in a distant city, a business acquaintance who was a devout practicing Catholic.

The two men dined together in the hotel that evening and then lingered long in the lobby talking business and politics. Finally, about eleven o'clock the Catholic arose and remarked that he must get some sleep, as he wanted to go out to Mass early the next morning. The sceptic then said to him, "It is really a puzzle to me, old man, if you will excuse my saying it, that a person of your intelligence and practicality, should see anything in that sort of thing. What is there about this Catholic religion that gets you in this way?"

In response to this hackneyed observation—which we Catholics often hear—his companion asked:

"What do *you* know about the Catholic religion?"

"Not a damned thing, except that it is an archaic type of Christianity long ago rejected by the more progressive Christian world. Really, I've never looked into it. Not that I'm prejudiced, but you know I'm not a Christian at all; not even a Protestant Christian, although I've often agreed with liberals in the pulpits who take sound stands on public questions. But just what is it that inspires a man like you to get up early and go out to church on a week day?"

"That question would require a long answer, and even if I talked all night it might not mean anything to you. But I suggest this. If you really want to know the answer, why not get up early tomorrow morning, and go out to Mass with me? There's a church just up the street. Perhaps you might get the best short answer to your question in that way."

To his surprise, the sceptic agreed and was promptly on hand the next morning. He had never been at a Catholic Mass before, and naturally it was all very strange to him. But he was deeply impressed by its mystic solemnity, as well as by the presence of so many devout people at this early hour of a week-day morning; and also, no doubt, by the devoutness of his companion.

On their way back to the hotel for breakfast, he asked, "Do you often go out to Mass on week days like this?"

"Every morning for the past twenty years—unless ill or where no church is within reach. It's the way I always start my day if I can."

To the agnostic that was a startling statement. It profoundly mystified him that any man should want to go to church every day—and before breakfast at that. And it silenced him too—he asked no more questions. But he thought a lot about it, both then and later. And from that time forward, when anything pertaining to the Catholic Church came to his attention, the words of his companion of that morning invariably came back to his mind—"Every morning for the past twenty years." . . .

Time rolled on, and this sceptic, restless and unsettled about many things, and particularly about the futility of life—as the sceptically minded who have no constructive philosophy often are—one day suddenly decided that it might be worthwhile to look a bit seriously into this baffling thing, Catholicism, which seemed to have the power to induce a hard-headed business man to go regularly to Mass every morning of his life. Surely there must be something in it not apparent on the surface.

He did look seriously into it. And what was the final result? As happens more often than some people realize, he ultimately became a Catholic himself—and a sincerely practicing one at that. Today this man knows the same peace and serenity he had detected in that chance meeting with his friend.

This man was once asked what other influences aside from being impressed by the Catholicity of his friend had inspired him to look into the Catholic Church. Were there not other incidents also that started him on his way?

"There were some minor incidents which may have influenced me," he said. "One of them still sticks in my memory. I happened to go some years ago on a brief business trip to South America. In the hotel where I was staying in Peru, I became acquainted with a Protestant missionary who seemed to be idle most of the time, evidently finding it hard to inoculate the Peruvians with his brand of Christianity. One Sunday morning he and I went out for a long walk in the country. We strolled along a dusty road many miles from the city limits. Far out on that road we passed a large group of men, women and children, all barefoot poor people. They were trudging towards the town. I asked my companion why it was that these obviously half starved and mostly ragged peasants all had such happy, smiling faces."

" 'Those people!' he explained, 'are going to church. They make this trek every Sunday morning. Some of them come from at least twenty miles away and must have started before dawn. You ask me why they all have such smiling faces? That question is easily answered—they are Catholics.' "

"Perhaps still other incidents influenced me from time to time; but it is unlikely that I would have been impressed had it not been for that first incident when I went to Mass with my business friend. It was, without doubt, the force of his example as a daily communicant—'every morning for the past twenty years'—which really started me on the road to the Church."

Now therein lies the true answer to the convert-making problem. It is the answer which every Catholic of apostolic or missionary zeal should not fail to take to heart; and especially the new convert who thinks he sees an eager prospect every time he turns a corner. You may never be able to accomplish very much through argument and disputation —but at least you can always "show them" by example!

CHAPTER SEVEN

THE GRIP ON REALITY

1.

"THE TROUBLE with you nowadays is that you have lost your grip on reality. And it's all because you have slid into the quagmire of religion. That's what the Catholic Church has done to you!"

These words were flung at me by an old-time Wall Street acquaintance, after an hour's discussion of his personal financial problems. His querulous remark was due to the fact that I had been unable to give him any very satisfactory advice as to how he was to get out of a financial hole into which he had deliberately jumped.

As is always my custom in such cases, I passed up his remark with a smile. I had heard it before. And then, almost on the heels of this sarcastic rap at my religion, another Wall Street man said to me:

"You have a far better grip on reality nowadays than you used to have. You are more logical, and not so easily duped. I suppose it's because you are a Catholic. I'm not a Catholic myself, as you know. Religion doesn't interest me. But I have long observed that Catholics, who *know why* they are Catholics, often turn out to be stronger on logic than some of the rest of us."

So there you are. Some Wall Street people are sure you have lost your grip on reality by embracing the Catholic

Faith, while others are sure you have found it for the first time. Is that surprising? Not at all. For you must remember that Wall Street is made up of the same miscellaneous sorts of human beings as the rest of society; wise men, mediocre men, stupid men; the shrewd, the dull, the honest and the dishonest. It is not at all unusual to find people there who contradict one another on every vital subject under the sun—including the meaning of reality.

A credulous outside public has been brought up on the fiction that there is but one school of Wall Street thought; a mercenary, hard-boiled, materialistic school. And despite the great eclipse of this financial center during the past decade, the fancy still seems to persist that if you are a Wall Street man there must be something cold-blooded, slick or tricky in your make-up. If you are prominent, you are always in danger of being pictured in the yellow journals as a money-soaked monopolist—even though you may be broke; if you are not prominent, you are likely to be permanently under suspicion of hiding ill-gotten gains, anyway. In any event, you are too smart, or too besmirched by economic royalist ideas, to be trusted.

Poor old Wall Street! It gets credit in the public mind for many things for which it is entitled to no credit; as well as blame for many things of which it is not guilty. For a full half century of my own experience, I have seen it condemned as the fountainhead of all financial crime; I have seen it defended as the source of many blessings. It has been roundly damned by men who have lost their money there, and fulsomely praised by lucky lambs who have walked away (and stayed away) with their speculative profits. I know many sober citizens, never trimmed in the speculative markets, who see the Street from afar as the one place in this country where men are sane and balanced, and where supermen are born and bred. And I have known—and still know—many others who have ever viewed it as the arch enemy of American society, and if not altogether a den of iniquity, at least the natural home of the utterly lawless and corrupt.

Of course this financial center has, and has always had, its share of rascals, as it has and always has had, its share of honest men. It has its bogus realists as well as its genuine ones. But as a community it is just a cross-section of average humanity—and just as inadequate as average humanity. Its proportion of brilliant minds is about the same as may be found in any field of endeavor—in big business or little business, in politics or in the professions. You can thrive or suffer in Wall Street and at the same time be a conservative or a reactionary, a radical, a New Dealer, a socialist or a communist—or almost anything else you wish to be. Franklin Roosevelt was a Wall Street product as well as Wendell Willkie. During my own half century there I played or toyed with both conservatism and radicalism, and many other intermediate isms; I did all this right in the face of the bulls and bears, and am still here to tell the tale.

2.

Far back near the close of the 1920's, well before I became a Catholic, I wrote an article on the economic confusion of the day, which was later published in the *Commonweal*, the well-known Catholic weekly. In that article I strongly criticised some aspects of the prevailing business corruption, suggesting that it was time for a return on the part of high financiers and fortune seekers, to life's verities.

That little article met with considerable criticism in certain quarters. I recollect the comment of one follower of the gospel of greed, who had piled up a fabulous fortune during the boom days and was then trying to prevent it from slipping through his fingers. With some indignation he said to me:

"That's an extraordinary view of business ethics you propounded in that *Commonweal* article. Do you mean to tell me that I have no right to do as I please with my own money; that I have no right to circumvent a law if it is a fool law? How can you say it is immoral for me to fool the government on my income tax—if I can get away with it? That's not evasion; that's avoidance. What becomes of my stockholders, my labor, if the government takes such a big slice of my legitimate income and profits that I must reduce dividends, or perhaps shut down my plant? And what becomes of me? Why man, if things went on like that I would soon stare poverty in the face!"

That was a dozen years ago. You don't hear speeches like that nowadays. But in the lurid days of the latter 1920's one heard plenty of such talk. That was the time when a certain type of "realism" was at its height. And it was not confined to Wall Street, although the wild speculation going on there did draw devotees of the gospel of greed from all across the country. During the late 1920's, many of our schools were training young men for financial careers, concentrating on the technique of high-pressure bond salesmanship. At the same time, investors from coast to coast flooded Wall Street with funds for use in getting rich quick; farmers mortgaged their farms, men and women everywhere hocked their life insurance policies, sold their Liberty bonds, drew down on their savings or borrowed money at the banks; politicians, reformers, labor leaders, and even some preachers of the Gospel, rushed funds to Wall Street. And for what purpose? Simply to share in what all Wall Street was thought to be doing—getting rich overnight.

It was a gala day for the gamblers, such as perhaps had not been known since the days of the famous South Sea Bubble in London during the first decade of the eighteenth century. Everybody was going to be rich, from the biggest of the big business man down to the bootblack and the panhandler; and this would settle every economic and social problem that had bothered mankind since the dawn of history. All Americans seemed to believe just that, during the last two years of the so-called Coolidge prosperity. So sound was the philosophy linked with the name of Calvin Coolidge considered to be, that his immediate successor in the White House, who tried to follow in his footsteps, intimated that poverty was shortly to be abolished in this land of the free and home of the brave.

It was indeed a New Era. But it was all very short. Greed had spread like a prairie fire among all classes throughout the country during that hectic period; but it culminated dramatically enough before the decade closed. And Wall Street, so widely advertised as the fountainhead of easy money, naturally got all the blame for what followed, and is still blamed. It was right that it should have suffered some of the blame, but I have never felt it deserved *all* the blame. For that period saw an immense extra supply of greed poured into its coffers from the rest of the country—and indeed from many other countries—which all but smothered and swamped the greed of its own manufacture. It has often been pointed out, with justice, that if Wall Street

dug its own grave during that lurid time, it certainly had
plenty of voluntary coöperation from a large army of outside grave-diggers.

Here is an objective illustration of the foregoing statement. A certain politician from out of the wild and woolly
west (a severe critic of the Wall Street wolves) made my
acquaintance early in the year 1928. Although a professional politician; he called himself a progressive reformer;
he was also a prime believer in the main chance. Sentimentality was not in his make-up; life to him was to get on; to
get on. And evidently, as a business politician there had
been considerable getting on, for he boasted of a very substantial bank account.

Now in the summer of 1927 this seasoned business politician began to envisage a halcyon period ahead for his beloved country—despite the strangle hold of big business on
the Coolidge administration, which he hated in true par-
tisan fashion. Accordingly he quietly withdrew from his
business at home a substantial amount of his capital. An
era of inflated values seemed to be in the making, being
especially foreshadowed by the steady rise in Wall Street
stocks. And with this capital he went into the Wall Street
stock market—incognito—to stake it on several sky rockets
just then about to shoot.

Luck was with him. Within less than a year thereafter
he had profits of over a hundred thousand dollars. But this
soon seemed a trivial sum compared to the fortunes then
building all around him, and before the opening of 1929 he
plunged into the market for "real money." During the ensuing nine or ten months he skimmed off gravy to his
heart's content, and by the early autumn of 1929 he had
cleaned up, "using my own brains and with no help from

the Wall Street highway robbers," as he boasted to me, nearly a million dollars. Of course, these fabulous winnings were mostly paper profits, for like all the bogus realists of that lurid time, he was loath to cash in; partly because of the high income taxes he would have to pay on his massive profits, but more because he knew he was on the broad highway to greater riches. He believed fervently in the timeworn proverb that "the first million is the hardest," and was sure that additional millions would now come easy.

Early in the month of October, 1929, this self-made super-realist divulged to me, in private conversation, not only the facts above recounted, but also his latest revised version of the near-by future of America. I shall here try to inscribe this brilliant confession of faith—this astounding grip on reality—in his own words, as accurately as I can now recall them.

"This wonderful era of prosperity we are now in the midst of," he declared, "is of course the fruit of the wise, far-seeing individualism so characteristic of us Americans. It is our healthy ambition to rise in the scale of life and to acquire the wherewithal to do it. This struggle for success is too deep-seated in us to be completely hamstrung by the rascals who are running things in Washington. What a blessing it is that our great American citizenship, despite the Washington thimbleriggers, has adhered to its well-balanced sanity; that sanity which has made this the greatest nation in all history, where a contented and happy people are ever-increasingly enjoying the benefits of peace and plenty.

"Yes, I know I am talking primarily of material progress; but this great record of ours is not merely material; there is a *spiritual tinge* in what we are doing today. For example, we haven't turned our backs on suffering Europe; we have been loaning her some of our money. American investors have been willing, even eager, to purchase foreign securities of every type. I own a goodly amount myself. No, we haven't been guilty of greed or selfishness; rather have we been inspired by brotherly sympathy for those less fortunate than ourselves, and wherever possible have extended a helping hand." (Is it necessary to say that rhetoric was no mean asset of this great realist?)

"In view of all this," he went on, "how can any sane person doubt that we are now but at the beginning of this period of progress and prosperity? Coming events cast their shadows before; the present Wall Street boom is but a foretaste, a foreshadowing, of still better things to come. I am not relying on the words of the man in the White House; he just happens to be right this once. But the facts are before our eyes. You may say as much as you like that my views are visionary; but they are echoed by many an expert, many an economist, many far-seeing industrial and financial leaders. There isn't even the proverbial small cloud on the horizon; the sky is clear in every direction. And so I say, it is wise to profit by these facts. Above all, let us be realists."

These words of wisdom, remember, were uttered in the first week of October, 1929. At that time all the bogus realists, both in and out of Wall Street, were busily at work pyramiding their paper profits to the limit. Everybody knew that the sky was not the roof; prices would go through the sky to infinity beyond.

Within two or three weeks after this oratorical effort had been spent on me, the great cataclysm of 1929 burst upon the country. The fabulous fortunes of all these bogus realists, little and big, were promptly blown to the four winds of heaven. Billions of dollars of fictitious values evaporated and faded out like the morning mist before the rising summer sun.

Like many of the other victims, my wordy friend struggled madly to save something from the wreck. But as with the vast majority, he made blunder after blunder in his plunges to save himself and was caught in the doghouse again and again. Before another year had elapsed, his entire fortune, as well as his faith in his bogus realism, had melted away, spiritual tinge and all. Even his original cash, made available when he embarked on his great adventure, was no more.

And it may as well be here recorded, by way of parenthesis, that his former legitimate business in the West, as well as his political prestige at home, had also completely collapsed, having died of negligence during his brief career of feverish effort to outdo Wall Street in super-acquisitiveness. Nor did he himself linger many years longer in this vale of tears. The Reaper soon came and mercifully closed the chapter.

It would be easy for me to recount many other incidents of this general character. But this one should be sufficient to point the moral—which is, that the morons of that hectic period were by no means *all* Wall Street men.

3.

One may correctly guess that the type of realist of the foregoing incident would surely tell me that I had lost my grip on reality as a result of becoming a Catholic. And as a matter of fact, the person I quoted at the beginning of this chapter was precisely this type; he held about the same views on things both human and divine. But as I also pointed out, another man who regarded himself as very realistic, made the more pleasing comment that I nowadays have a better grip on reality as a result of being a Catholic. You might assume that this latter person must have known something about Catholicism, even if he were not a Catholic himself. But you would be wrong in that assumption.

There are plenty of men in Wall Street, as elsewhere, who are genuine realists and who know all about the Catholic religion, whether they believe it or live it or not. More about that class later. But this person who made this kindly remark, was simply one of those hard-boiled money grubbers of native shrewdness, quite characteristic of American business life, whose whole preoccupation is the acquisition of dollars and cents. They are usually very uninteresting men; but they seldom spend much time indulging in prejudices, and generally have little hate in their hearts. They are usually tolerant of everything—provided it does not interfere with or divert their attention from their own mercenary activities.

This particular hard head, now deceased, was, when he made the kindly remark about my new grip on reality, the president of a financial institution. By relating the appended incident I can picture him (as well as some of his business associates) far more vividly than by any attempt at detailed description.

It happened that I was present as his guest at a luncheon with his board of directors and a few others. The conversation ranged widely over various financial topics; and then, as we relaxed over our coffee at the end, one of the directors remarked to the man opposite him that he be-

lieved in the immortality of the soul—an unusual subject
to bring up at a luncheon of captains of industry. As the
oracle raised his voice—his listener opposite being a little
deaf—all present stopped to listen. Then the president
called out from the end of the table, ten feet away:

"Talking about immortality? That's religion, isn't it?
That should interest our friend Moody; he believes in it.
He's a Catholic, you know."

"Oh, I don't mean that sort of immortality," the oracle
explained. "The Catholics say you go *personally* to some
place they call Heaven—just as you might pack up and
go to Europe. They say you will meet your family and
loved ones there. I never could swallow that nonsense.
Anyhow, there are plenty of dead ones I don't want to
meet again. But at the same time I hold that there *is* something beyond this life for our souls, even though it's hard
to imagine just what it is. Certainly it cannot be personal
survival as taught by the Catholics—with all due respect
to Mr. Moody. But when we die, while we know that the
body decays and so that's the end of that, our soul surely
goes on. We must not forget that we have souls as well as
bodies. Oh yes, we have! (This to the man on his left who
contradicted him here.) Our souls must continue to exist
in some form. But what form? Ah, there's the rub. Have
any of you ever read any occult philosophy? You should.
It's deep. Take, for instance, the Over Soul idea of Emerson."

"Oversold idea? How do you mean—oversold?" broke
in the president. "I doubt if the Emerson Drug company
ever have been so fixed that they were overselling their
product. They know there is an unlimited demand for

bromo-seltzer, and you can bet they always have a big reserve supply on hand."

"Over *Soul*—not oversold," hastily explained the oracular one. "I'm not talking about bromo-seltzer, but about Emerson, the writer. Haven't you ever read Emerson? But it doesn't matter. I am thinking of the transmigration of souls—first suggested, I think, by the philosopher Pythagoras, thousands of years ago."

"Never heard of him," broke in the president.

"You wouldn't. But the idea is that your soul never dies; in fact, it never began; it always was. It comes back to earth again and again in new bodies. So you see you are born again; you have another shot at life; in fact, millions of shots——"

"What?" exclaimed the president. "Come back to this earth—this HELL we live in—millions of times? None of that for me. I'd like the Catholic idea better than that—purgatory, where you have one good chance, they tell me. Isn't that so, Moody? And if it's to hell you go—well, it's only once. . . . And the hell you get couldn't be worse than the hell we have right here. But tell me, what becomes of your soul, according to your crazy idea, after it stops being born again? Or doesn't it ever stop?"

"Surely, some day it stops, but only after you have reached perfection; after millions of births, perhaps. And then you have peace—eternal peace. You become a drop in the great ocean of peace. And that's called Nirvana. Oh, it's a deep philosophy. Better look into it."

It seemed time for me to say something. "Well," I ventured, "I for one *have* looked into it. I once prowled around in theosophy, esoteric Buddhism and other forms of the so-called 'occult'; so much so that I long ago discovered that your 'Nirvana' is nothing but annihilation of all personality. The short cut to this 'Nirvana' is atheism. So why go through millions of births to be finally annihilated? Atheism does that for you on the spot."

"That's what I say," exclaimed the man who had denied we have souls. "Atheism is the only logical view to take."

"You are wrong there," I interposed. "There are *two* logical views of human life, not one. And both depend on the basic premises. If you believe the Christian premise of the origin, nature and destiny of man; that man is a composite being of soul and body, created by Almighty God for an immortal destiny, then *Catholicism* is the only logical and rational philosophy of life. But if you believe that man is simply a glorified ape, that he evolved from dead matter, somehow grabbing life out of the air, then *atheism* is the logical view."

A profound silence followed that declamation. The atheist beamed; the Nirvana devotee scowled; some of the others stirred in their seats, but no one attempted to debate the point. Finally, one of the more elderly of the group broke the silence.

"All this talk about religion takes me back to my boyhood days, when my dad offered me two dollars to read the Bible through; and I won the two dollars. But when I told him I found the Bible full of contradictions, he, being a liberal sort of Christian, willingly admitted that it *was* mostly fables. And that was the end of religion for me."

"Of course," said I, "the Bible confuses rather than enlightens unless interpreted by the authority which first gave it to the world—the Catholic Church."

"Is that where the Bible came from?" inquired the most

junior—and illiterate—director of the group. "I have never looked it up, nor read much of it. But I've always understood it was compiled, or at least translated, by old King James of England. Isn't it called the King James Bible? But what you are telling us now is brand new to me. So the Catholic Church gave us the Bible? How do the Protestants get around that?"

From this point I was proceeding, in missionary fashion, to drive home a few Catholic facts; but as I glanced around the table, watches were being sprung on me. It was time for these captains of industry to get back to business.

Probably little aside from the bromo-seltzer incident remained with that group after they had emerged into the air. But as I bid my host good-by a few moments later, he remarked by way of apology that the luncheon had wound up like a prayer meeting. And then he added:

"You mustn't take our oversold friend too seriously; he's always trying to spring some crazy idea. Ought to keep his mind on business, I say. Just imagine you and me wanting to come back to this earth millions of times—so we could be a drop in some ocean!"

4.

I trust the foregoing story will not convey the impression that these men were typical Wall Street realists. They were indeed quite exceptional. There are to be found plenty of men of genuine intelligence in the financial world; many who would perhaps surprise you by their knowledge of numerous things aside from the almighty dollar; men who have a firm grip on genuine reality, who have rational reasons for their thoughts and beliefs; are fully capable of giving sound reasons for the faith that is in them. In fact, I have more than once made the statement that it was basically because of my own Wall Street life that I was ultimately led to the door of the Catholic Church. And there is more truth than poetry in that statement; for I surely learned, during my years in that field of endeavor, how to reason from causes to effects, how to dig to fundamentals and be sure they were fundamentals, and thus to arrive at safe, logical conclusions.

Not that I mean to imply that my business life was ever marked by any degree of perfection; my entire business career, like that of everyone else, has just naturally been a comedy of errors. But as also in the cases of many others, I did learn something through trial and error, and particularly to apply a principle which had been driven deeply into my consciousness in my earliest days of business life. That principle is—seek for basic facts; know you are right before you go ahead.

A somewhat amusing incident in the days of my youth will illustrate what I mean by the importance of first knowing basic facts or premises. Far back in the year 1890, when I first went into Wall Street as a mere errand boy, I was one day sent by my employers to the office of Drexel, Morgan & Company (later J. P. Morgan & Company) to deliver a large package of railroad bonds amounting in value to something between fifty and fifty-five thousand dollars. I was to get a check in payment for these bonds. The exact amount of the payment to be made was clearly marked on the envelope containing the bonds; but I had carelessly failed to make note of this amount when handing the bonds to the cashier at the window. I simply said I would wait for the check. The cashier took the package from me and then disappeared with it into a room at the rear.

Now in those days J. Pierpont Morgan (the elder) was the active head of that firm. He had a habit of often strolling through the office and sometimes glancing over the shoulders of the clerks while they were at work. And this particular morning it happened that he stepped into the cashier's cage just as the latter disappeared with the package of bonds. Mr. Morgan, a very large man with a red, bulbous nose, and with powerful eyes which seemed to bore through one, glanced at me (a timid little kid of twenty-one) as I peered over the counter, obviously in great trepidation. That was indeed my exact state, for the cashier had taken the bonds and disappeared, and I had begun to wonder if I would get the check. (Of course, the cashier was simply having the bonds counted before drawing and paying over the check. But in my innocence I never thought of that.)

After staring at me a moment or two, Mr. Morgan, who was also awaiting the cashier's return, burrowed his great eyes through me and asked:

"What's the matter, sonny?"

"Nothing—nothing," I replied in a tremulous tone; "I'm just waiting for a check for some bonds I have delivered to the cashier."

"What is the amount of the check you are to receive?" asked Mr. Morgan.

Having failed to note the exact figure, I hesitated, and then ventured, "It is something between fifty and fifty-five thousand; I don't remember exactly."

"Don't remember?" roared Mr. Morgan. "What kind of

a messenger are you? You have been sent here with a package of great value, for which you are to get a check; and you don't remember how much you are to get? Suppose we should cheat you? What could you do about it? Young man, let me tell you something. You will never get anywhere in life; you will never amount to a hill of beans, unless you learn to know *basic facts*. And the exact amount of that check you are to receive is at this moment the basic fact for you."

Just then the cashier returned with the check. Mr. Morgan grabbed it, glanced at it and read out the amount— $53,425.70. "Is that correct?" he asked me.

Naturally I said it was. He glowered, and then said, before handing me the check, "How do you know it is the correct amount? *You don't know!* Now remember what I told you; never go off half-cocked; know your facts beforehand."

Although a half century has since gone by, I have never forgotten a single detail of that incident—not even the amount of the check. Nor the moral which it conveyed. And although I often failed to adhere to the advice about knowing my facts beforehand—and consequently suffered —yet the principle I never completely forgot.

And so it was that when, in later years, searching for the deeper things of life by looking into various theories and philosophies, it was the basic principles which sooner or later were searched for, rather than superficial aspects. In my young manhood, I toyed with all sorts of phases of modern thought, with "liberal" brands of Christianity and various forms of pantheism; but none of these things gripped me for long, for I instinctively searched for their sources and basic premises, and was always sooner or later disillusioned. Not until I found Catholicism did this test hold.

You see what I mean therefore, when I say that my Wall Street experience had something to do with my embracing the Catholic Faith. I might go further and say that J. P. Morgan, the elder, had something to do with it. That may sound grotesque to some readers, for Mr. Morgan was anything but a Catholic. But I knew a lot about him before his demise in 1913. He had his faults, made many a mistake himself, and his outlook on life in general was quite different from that of many of us. But he surely did possess certain sound traits which are all too weak with the vast majority of fortune seekers.

Incidentally, I might say that the elder J. P. Morgan was the shrewdest judge of personal character in business life that I have ever known. And he certainly tried to govern his own business dealings with full recognition of the character of those he dealt with. Well do I recall an incident of one of the Wall Street crashes of those days. A certain brokerage concern was dangerously near failure. To save themselves they needed to borrow half a million dollars, but their credit was exhausted with the banks and they had little available collateral for a loan of this amount. In desperation the head of this firm went personally to Morgan, laid his cards on the table, frankly showing his weak position and his inability to raise sufficient collateral. Yet he must have the money if his firm was not to fail the next day.

Mr. Morgan, who was a man of quick decision, said to him: "Never mind about the collateral; I will take your word that you are good for the loan. You may have the money. I am loaning it on your character—which I know."

The firm was saved; and in due course the loan was repaid.

On the other hand, also during a panic, a concern of doubtful character applied to Morgan for a loan of several millions, at a high rate of interest and with ample security of prime quality. But it is said that Morgan instantly refused; the essential thing—character—was lacking.

All that is a side of J. P. Morgan's personality which writers of polemics against Wall Street don't spare much space to tell us about. One may not have agreed with J. P. Morgan in a lot of his practices or policies in his long business career; but it is well to remember that he did understand the value of character.

And so I repeat that there was something fundamental in my Wall Street experience which favorably affected my own course when the time came for me to "look into" the Catholic religion. I was governed to a very large extent by that habit of first going to the root of things; of seeking the basic facts before going ahead. That early lecture to me through the Morgan cashier's window was—and still is—potent.

5.

Right here I am reminded of another incident. I hope my readers are not growing weary of incidents in this book; but those who are had better toss it out of the window now, for many more are to follow as we go on.

This incident relates to St. Paul the Apostle, whom I also discovered by way of Wall Street. And I like to write about him; for he has not only been my most enlightening guide during my life in the Catholic Church, but he had much to do, in a certain sense, in starting me along the road to the Church.

During my pagan days of the 1920's, it was long my custom to go down to business on the Ninth Avenue Elevated road, and often, as the train passed Fifty-ninth Street, I would notice a mammoth canvas sign stretched over the entrance of the immense basilica which covers the block between Fifty-ninth and Sixtieth streets. It is the Church of St. Paul the Apostle. The sign was always headed, MISSIONS TO NON-CATHOLICS, and listed a series of addresses to be delivered by various Paulist priests. It seemed odd to me that any intelligent persons would be attracted by that sort of thing; certainly no hard-boiled business men who had a firm grip on reality. What sort of people responded to appeals like that? Perhaps the emotional and superstitious. Nevertheless, as time went on, I found myself watching out for these signs with growing interest.

Then one day a certain Wall Street man that I knew intimately and had always regarded as quite hard-boiled, surprised me by saying that he had been going to some of these Paulist lectures that winter, had learned a lot, and urged me to try it out myself if I was interested in learning something fundamental about Christianity. "You will be surprised to find," he said, "that there is really something *basic* to this Catholic religion; basic facts which most of us overlook and know nothing about. It is not a mere emotional appeal; they really do give you something to think about."

But of course I wouldn't "try it out." Go into a Catholic church? That sort of thing simply wasn't done in my world. But notwithstanding, I continued to read these bulletins with interest all that winter; an interest which was greatly accelerated when, later on, my Wall Street, hard-boiled friend bowled me over by suddenly becoming a Catholic himself.

How did this startling event react on me? It meant that a Wall Street man whose grip on reality I had always considered as being unusually strong, had either grown mentally soft with his advancing years, or really had found something. Several talks with him followed and my curiosity was sufficiently whetted to soon induce me, despite all my inbred prejudices, to slip over to the Paulist church alone one Sunday evening.

The church was thronged. I was squeezed into a seat far to one side, a long distance from the pulpit. There was very fine singing by the Paulist choir; very little else aside from the sermon, which was preached by a young man of great eloquence, Reverend Fulton J. Sheen, of the Catholic University in Washington. His sermon quite intrigued me; there was nothing emotional or sentimental about it; it was marked by clear logical reasoning. And at the end I had to admit to myself that there was something underlying this Catholic religion which looked suspiciously like truth itself.

Crowded to one side, I could see little of the sanctuary; but on the opposite wall of the vast basilica and directly in my line of vision, was a large painting of the martyrdom of St. Paul, with the following inscription in very large letters.

> I have fought the good fight;
> I have finished my course;
> I have kept the Faith.

My eyes were glued on that painting and on that inscription all through the sermon and afterwards until I departed. And with those words haunting me, when I got home that evening, I went to our old family Bible and read a great gob of St. Paul's Epistles and the Acts—for the first time, perhaps, in more than thirty years. I recollect that the clock struck one, struck two, before I laid the Bible aside. I had found this far more interesting reading than my daily dose of financial dope.

That was the birth of a keen interest in St. Paul which has steadily increased through the years. Perhaps during the past decade I have read more about St. Paul, and have become more familiar with his influence on early Christian dogma, than may be the case with many others, Catholic or non-Catholic. If, indeed, I have the grip on genuine realities which I believe I have, it is in large measure due to my efforts to understand and keep in correct perspective the mind and life of this first great convert to the Christian Faith.

And, you see, the genesis of that was Wall Street!

6.

There was one other incident during the days when I had little notion that in my search for genuine realities, my Wall Street environment would help to lead me towards the Catholic Church.

About the time my friend had surprised me by his conversion, it happened that I was reading a short history of the reign of Henry VIII, written by Francis Hackett. There was considerable in this book regarding Sir Thomas More's attitude towards the king's effort to divorce Queen Catherine. Up to that time my impression of Sir Thomas More was that he must have been a foolhardy person to be willing to go to the block for a mere papal superstition. That was the opinion I expressed to a certain Wall Street man, who was himself something of a student of English history and whose antecedents were English.

To my surprise this man did not agree with me that Sir Thomas More had been foolhardy. While we did not argue the point to any extent at that time, he called my attention to another book on the subject of More's controversy, and asked me to read it in order to get a full and accurate version of the struggle between Sir Thomas and his king.

I secured a copy of this book and read it. When I had finished I was convinced that Sir Thomas More was not only a saint, but a man of definitely objective mind who reasoned to basic facts. He had a splendid grip on the realities, both human and divine. When he stood before the judge and jury which condemned him, these were his words:

"I have, by the grace of God, been always a Catholic, never out of communion with the Roman Pontiff; but I have heard it said at times that the authority of the Roman Pontiff was certainly lawful and to be respected, but still an authority derived from human law, and not standing upon a divine prescription. Then, when I observed that public affairs were so ordered that the sources of the power of the Roman Pontiff would necessarily be examined, I gave myself up to a diligent examination of that question for the space of seven years, and found that the authority of the Roman Pontiff, which you rashly—I will not use stronger language—have set aside, is not only lawful to be respected and necessary, but also grounded on the divine law and prescription. That is my opinion, that is the belief in which, by the Grace of God, I shall die."

That statement of More's, made as he entered death's door, lodged so securely in my memory, that soon thereafter I also gave myself up to a diligent study of this question of the Papal supremacy. And when I had finished digging down to the facts of the matter, the evidence in support of the divine authority of the Roman Pontiff was as convincing to me as it had been to St. Thomas.

And so, after all, it is a mistake to say that a grip on reality cannot be found in Wall Street. In this chapter I started out with mordant irony regarding certain types in Wall Street who claim to have a grip on reality. But I hope I am ending by showing that a genuine grip on reality can be found there was well as elsewhere. For it was in that reputedly murky atmosphere that I learned, as a digger out of facts, to go to the foundations of things, to seek for fundamental premises, to learn how *not* to confuse causes and effects. In short, to learn, to some degree at least, how to avoid the pitfalls of life and to be able now and then to pick the wheat from the chaff.

*   *   *

In my early Catholic days I happened to be present one evening at a dinner given by some Catholic organization. Two men at a near-by table (who were obviously not aware that I was within earshot) were talking about me. One of them had this to say:

"It's a mystery to me that this man of the world, after spending a lifetime in Wall Street, should suddenly do such a startling thing as to become a Catholic." And the other had replied:

"Life is full of mysteries like that. But this is a new one. I've heard of converts coming out of Protestant pulpits and out of schools and colleges; I've heard of them coming out of coal mines and out of ditches—but never before have I heard of a convert coming out of Wall Street. What do you suppose is the answer to that?"

This chapter is the answer.

Chapter Eight

NOT SO BAD, AFTER ALL

I.

DURING YOUR EARLY CONVERT YEARS you are only too likely to talk rashly in an authoritative tone regarding Catholic doctrines and dogmas; especially to those outside the fold that you think know far less about these matters than you do yourself. And you are sure to get into trouble. People will ask you unexpected questions which you cannot answer correctly; or perhaps not at all. Not only will you be likely to give them inadequate answers; but sometimes you will give the wrong answers. It is a risky business, this habit of setting yourself up as an authority.

For instance, you will be apt to overlook the fact that different persons mean different things when asking the same question; or their interpretations of your answers will vary. Sometimes they will quote you as being the authority for statements which you are conscious of never having made at all.

A case in point. I once tried to explain to a supposedly intelligent person that the present reigning Pope is the latest of an unbroken line of pontiffs extending all the way back to St. Peter. I recall that he expressed astonishment, but I thought he understood what I meant—until some time later I learned he was telling people that the present Pius XII is a lineal *family* descendant of St. Peter, and quoting me as the authority!

When I told this incident to a lay Catholic acquaintance, he immediately said, "Never try to explain things like that; don't stick your neck out."

Yet what are you going to do when the Faith is assailed and maligned, or the Church is made a subject of ridicule in your hearing or among your friends? If you are to stand up for your beliefs when it clearly is your duty to do so, you are bound to at least state the truth as you see it, regardless of the way others may distort your words. But— you should know what you are talking about.

Ignorance and prejudice always breed intolerance. The average person who is violently anti-Catholic is usually profoundly ignorant of Catholicism. Many of the criticisms of the Church, of her doctrines and dogmas and her discipline, display an ignorance and a credulity which are scarcely conceivable of intelligent people. Writers of books, scholars and teachers, who on any other subject try to be meticulously accurate, will sometimes make the most astoundingly absurd statements about the Catholic religion; and often quite obviously without having made the slightest effort to check up on their statements or investigate the subject at all.

Unfortunately hosts of honest and sincere people will readily believe those who claim to speak with authority but have no authority at all. Yet this state of things will prevail forever if all Catholics follow the policy of never "sticking their necks out." If you don't know the answer to a false statement, you can at least insist that there is an answer— and then go and look the answer up. You may be too stupid to dig it out yourself; but if so, you can always find a priest who is likely to have it on the tip of his tongue.

At the same time, the individual Catholic is likely to do

more harm than good if he is himself intolerant and uncharitable towards those who rail against the Faith. Converts, during their early militant stage, often forget this. I recall the case of a convert who, before he had entered the Church, and while still attached to a Protestant sect (but in a state of doubt) asked his minister to tell him why he should not become a Catholic. The minister said it was merely a case of "Roman fever" and that he would soon get over it; but promised to make an appointment later to discuss the subject in detail. Time went on, the minister failed to make any appointment—it probably had slipped his mind—and shortly thereafter his unsettled parishioner entered the Catholic Church. He then wrote at once to the minister resigning from the Protestant body, but added at the end of his letter the following caustic comment:

"I know now why you never made that appointment to discuss matters with me. You were *afraid* to discuss the subject, for you know well enough that you had no argument; that the Catholic Church is right and you are wrong!"

Later on the convert mentioned that uncharitable act to a priest—it was on his conscience—and, as he told me, "The priest gave me a long lecture on the sins of intolerance and uncharitableness."

All this came forcibly to my mind a year or two ago when the letter quoted below came to me. Here is a person who doesn't hesitate to stick his neck out—very far out. When he wrote this letter he had probably just come into the Church, and knew all too little about the virtue of charity. So belligerently and rudely does he express himself that I am afraid some austere, unimaginative Catholics —not to say pagans or non-Catholics—will jump to the conclusion that the letter was composed by myself as a springboard for plunging into the sea of religious controversy. But not so. This gem of militant writing came to me through the mail. It was signed, in very bold letters, A MILITANT CONVERT. Here are some excerpts from it.

Won't you please write a ripping good Catholic book to convert the pagans all around us? . . . Of course, if in their pigheaded assurance, the pagans get any inkling that what you tell them is right, they may lay the book aside and try to forget it the best way they can. For while they will sense that what you say is right, they don't want their reason or intellect (or whatever they use to make thoughts out of) to tell them —to *insist* to them—that they must follow you through to the logical conclusion. Because they will see at once it would mean that they must go to Church with a lot of mixed crowds, early in the morning, even before breakfast, and so get upset stomachs. And worse than that, they will see that they must tell a priest, a mere man, their sins. (As if they could have any sins—huh!).

I think these two Items keep thousand of pagans and Protestants from allowing their curiosity full swing by even sticking their noses into a Catholic church.

Now you are a smart fellow, and if you will write something for the Pagan World which will pour soothing hot oil on these Items, so that the Pagan World will be willing to satisfy itself that these Items are not so bad after all, you will be one of the Great Catholics, a very, very Great One.

No Catholic, aside from an extremely raw convert, would write a screed like that. But to think that he should pick on me as the instrument for pouring soothing hot oil on these items. What a reputation for caustic controversy I must have built up! I think of the old adage—give a dog a bad name, and so on. . . .

Still, in spite of his intolerant language, this person has, in a sense, hit the nail on the head. These *are* "items" that are widely viewed by many as being decisive objections to Catholicism. There is no doubt about it. But the average non-Catholic would express himself less crudely and certainly less intolerantly. He would be likely to put his objections more as follows:

(Item One) "The horrible mixture of people you must rub shoulders with in Catholic churches, belittles or endangers your social standing; and the requirement of early rising to go to Mass on an empty stomach, undermines your health and ruins your digestion."

(Item Two) "The slavish superstition of allowing priests to put themselves between you and your God, weakens your character and makes you a cringing coward. Moreover, if you tell your sins to a priest, he learns exactly what you are guilty of and so gets a strangle hold on you."

Now while I have no capacity and no desire to "write a ripping good Catholic book to convert the pagans all around us"; nor any ambition to be "one of the great Catholics, a very, very great one," yet it may be worth while to pour a little soothing hot oil on these items, with the hope of showing that they are not so bad after all. A modest attempt to do this follows.

2.

As to the first item—relating to the horrible mixture of people you must rub shoulders with in Catholic churches. I shall approach this by telling of two personal experiences. And let me say that I am doing this in no spirit of venom or criticism; with no intention of questioning the good will or good faith of anybody. It is purely a statement of facts.

Back in my pre-Catholic days I went one bright Sunday to a large city church where a very "liberal" type of Christianity was supposed to be preached—modern "humanism." There was nothing exclusive about this church —except perhaps in the minds of some of its devotees. Everybody, regardless of social standing, of creed, race or color, was WELCOME—according to a neat little sign displayed at the entrance to the church.

I was a stranger; it was the first and only time I ever went there. The church was very large, very beautiful, and must have had a seating capacity of at least two thousand people. But it was more than half empty on my arrival a few moments before the service was to begin. The first thing I noticed was that a large group of people were standing in the rear, apparently being held in a sort of huddle by two or three ushers. These were obviously poor people, most of them shabby; and some of them looked poverty-stricken. Obviously they were all strangers like myself. I picked my way through this group and was about to proceed up the center aisle to one of the vacant pews, when one of the well-tailored, carnation-adorned ushers stopped me and smilingly asked, "Are you a pewholder?" On my replying in the negative his smile vanished as he said:

"You will have to stand in the rear during the first ten minutes of the service. The sittings are reserved for pewholders that long. After that I will give you a seat."

The ten minutes went by, during which only a handful more of the pewholders arrived; and then the ushers gave some of those still standing in the back of the church, seats in the rear pews, and I was one of those thus favored. But the bulk of the obviously poor and painfully shabby were hustled up to the gallery in the rear. The main body of the church was still half empty.

Did I get any spiritual uplift out of that experience? Not much. The music was fine and the preacher was eloquent, his text being taken from the parable of the pharisee and the publican; and he handled the subject well. But about all I could think of, while sitting there in the rear pew with a heavy pillar obstructing my view, and with that great array of good empty seats in front of me, was this: "In the comfortable and well located pews far to the front are . . . well, let us assume they are all good Christians. But all the publicans are crowded into these back pews, or packed upstairs in the gloomy and uncomfortable gallery."

So much for that experience. A stormy Sunday somewhat later I went to a Catholic church in the same city. The music was fine and the preaching also of a high order. It was a very large church, but was packed almost to the doors when I arrived about ten minutes early. Not a pew was vacant and scores of people were standing in the rear. I worked my way through this standing crowd, and then noticed that several ushers—*sans* carnations—were busily engaged in trying to find sittings here and there for the standees, by packing closer those already in the pews. As it happened, I was one of the fortunate ones, being led far to the front and packed in, sardine-like, between two very fat women. The pew was filled far beyond its normal capacity, with several children squeezed in very tightly. Aside from myself, there were surely no pharisees in that pew; they were all honest-to-God Catholic Christians.

Did I get any spiritual uplift out of this second experience? I did indeed. The fat men and women, old and young, and not excepting the tightly squeezed children, all put me to shame by their obvious sincerity, their reverence and devotion. They were not afraid to get down on their knees, nor to join in the singing at Benediction with great audibility. One felt that one was sandwiched in with a pewful of saints. These surely were God's children.

That, I think, should be sufficient soothing hot oil for the first point raised in Item One. But let us dwell a bit on the other point in that Item—the alleged obligation of Catholics to go to church every Sunday and also on some other days "early in the morning, even before breakfast" —thus running the risk of undermining health and ruining digestion.

The truth is that Catholics are *not* obligated to go to church "early in the morning, even before breakfast"; but a vast number of them freely choose to do this. You nearly always find more people at early Low Masses, than you do at late High Masses with their more elaborate ritual. The plainer the Mass the better the average Catholic likes it. To the average the elaborate ritual of High Mass is not particularly alluring; it is of slight importance compared to what the Catholic really goes to church for. He goes, not to enjoy music or hear long sermons, but to join with the priest in offering the Holy Sacrifice of the Mass, and also to receive Holy Communion. Let any non-Catholic step into a large city church at an early hour of any Sunday morning, or on the first Friday of any month, or on a Feast Day like All Saints, and he will certainly be impressed by the crowds of people who go up to the Communion rails.

Catholics are under no "obligation" to receive Holy Communion more frequently than once a year at Easter time. But the great majority of them do receive right along of their own volition, especially on the first Fridays; many every week, many several times a week, and a large number every morning.

There is also the grotesque notion, which seems to persist despite its absurdity, that Catholic churches are only crowded with the faithful because the latter are taught to fear their priests, who are ever threatening them with "the wrath of God," if they miss Mass. In short, there is a notion abroad that the religious life of the Catholic is built on a foundation of fear. A few years ago a prominent preacher stated from his pulpit, when upbraiding his congregation for lax attendance at church. "As an example of well filled churches I would point to the Catholics, were it not for the fact that they are a flock of sheep, driven to church through fear engendered by their priests."

Laughable! Perhaps a good answer to that is that Catholics surely are a flock of sheep, but they are not driven, they are led; led by the Good Shepherd, Who laid down His life for His sheep.

As for the Catholic custom of early rising and fasting "undermining one's health and ruining one's digestion," all I will say here is that since becoming a Catholic ten years ago my own chronic indigestion has entirely disappeared.

3.

Now for the "superstition" of confessing one's sins to a priest—a "mere man"; the other Item of this indictment. This may be worthy of a more extended discussion, for it sinks down in many minds as the major objection to Catholicism. In fact, with nearly all Protestants (except the High Church Episcopalians or "Anglo-Catholics") the very idea of confessing one's sins to a priest rather than "directly to

God," is utterly abhorrent. "I might find it not impossible to become a Catholic, were it not for two things—belief in hell and going to confession." That is the way it was once put to me by a pious Protestant.

A certain Protestant Episcopal minister said to me some years ago, during a conversation touching on the Sacrament of Penance as taught by the Catholic Church, "I have long believed in the efficacy of confessing one's sins. In fact, as a clergyman of my own church, I have often heard confessions. But I do not approve of the Catholic confessional box method."

On my asking him to explain his own method, he admitted that he had no regular method; he didn't believe in "standardizing" so solemn an act. Confession should be informal and made as easy as possible for the penitent, he said. And he made the following extraordinary comment.

"I understand that the Catholic method is to require a person to go into a confessional box, get on his knees and then tell a man behind a grille or screen the most intimate secrets of his soul—and all in the dark at that. That, I say, is ghoulish; it's as cold as ice. Why, man alive, there's no personal touch at all; not even a chance for a smile or a handshake."

—Nor, it might be added, for a smoke or a drink. If my friend had only added that touch, his comment would have been a classic. But truth compels me to admit that he didn't go that far.

Anyhow, his idea of confession, as he later explained it to me, was for a penitent to call by appointment at the pastor's study, where he would get a cordial welcome and be invited to spill his troubles in a friendly way. The pastor and penitent would "talk things over," the pastor treating the penitent as "an equal," thus bracing him up and helping him to retain his self-respect. And then, in closing, the pastor would change the subject to "lighter themes," finally sending the penitent away in peace and "quite consoled."

Very plausible. However, if we know anything about human nature, we must agree that few men would be likely to stroll into a minister's study, drop into an easy chair, casually reach for the proffered cigarette, and then in response to the inquiring smile of the cleric, blurt this out: "Doc, I've trimmed my employer out of a cool thousand, and it's on my conscience";—or, "I've gotten in trouble with a woman. What's to do about it?"

Would it not be far simpler for that man to confess his sin to a person behind a grille, whom he could not see and who could not see or identify him? Not only would it be far simpler, but it would be far more likely that the penitent one would go to confession.

4.

One may call the above comments frivolous. They are. But many a truth is spoken in jest, and it is good Catholic practice to sometimes picture the humorous side of things, and then change the tempo to a more serious vein. This we will now undertake to do.

What is really necessary before one passes judgment on the Catholic custom of going to confession, is a little understanding of the Catholic doctrine of grace. Passing references to this doctrine have been made on previous pages, but it might be worthwhile to explain it in a little more detail.

Now divine grace, as taught by Christ Himself and elucidated by St. Paul and later by St. Augustine, is a free gift of God and implies participation in the supernatural life of God. If one were to possess supernatural life in its completeness, that would mean nothing short of Heaven. In this connection it is sometimes said that a still living saint on earth is already partly in Heaven. The meaning of that metaphor is that the saint in question is blessed with sanctifying grace (the supernatural life) to a marked degree.

But of course the supernatural life in its completeness cannot be possessed by any of us in this world—we are all too weak, too "wounded" in our nature for that. It is this inherent weakness or "fault" in our human nature that first came about through the Fall of Man—what is theologically called Original Sin. This doctrine of grace, it will be seen, is directly linked to the Christian doctrine of the Fall of Man—as Catholics define the Fall, not as Calvinism did or does.

God's creative purpose was to place man on earth as a creature sharing in His supernatural life. He endowed man with intellect, free-will and immortality; attributes, of course, of Himself. In this sense, man was created in His image. Now free-will implies that one possesses freedom of choice; and Adam (who must be viewed here not as a mere individual, but as embracing the entire human race which stems from him), chose to disobey his creator. His punishment, as God had warned him, was the loss of his supernatural attributes; that is to say, of sanctifying grace. "Adam fell from grace," as Scripture puts it, meaning that he incurred a fault in his nature for himself and all his descendants, involving weakness of intellect and will, of soul and body, so that henceforth he was strongly inclined to "concupiscence," or sin. Hence the term, original sin.

All men who know themselves and are conscious of the

world about them, know that all humanity is weak in will and wholly inadequate to cope alone with its tendency to sin. Only pride prevents us from admitting to ourselves this all too obvious fact. Glance at the world today; at the holocaust which has overspread civilization. Is not our world wallowing in sin?

Now the Catholic teaching is that through the Sacrament of Christian Baptism—ordained by Christ Himself— we are endowed anew with certain of the attributes which Adam, for himself and for us, lost through sin. Christ's coming as our Redeemer did that for us. He endowed mankind anew with supernatural sanctifying grace. But as with Adam, this "life made new," which we receive in Baptism, is easily forfeited by us through our sins. Yet this endowment of grace need not be lost forever; we can always return, have "another chance," if we but will. And the primary method ordained by Christ for recovering sanctifying grace, is through the Sacrament of Penance.

Thus we have the spectacle of Catholic humanity all over the world (largely weak and faltering humans struggling through life), often lapsing from, in whole or in part, this endowment of grace, this "life made new"—and then recovering it through sincere contrition and confession. When the Catholic examines his conscience and realizes that he has committed some grievous sin, he goes to confession, confessing his sins to Almighty God through the instrument of the priest, at the same time making a sincere act of contrition and performing a penance given to him by the priest. If he does this in the right spirit—with the right intention—he will be absolved from his sin; and thus, being now in a "state of grace," will thereafter be free to receive Holy Communion. And Holy Communion, when devoutly received, of course further increases sanctifying grace in his soul.

Perhaps it might be here emphasized (for the benefit of non-Catholic readers) that the efficacy of absolution is measured by the genuineness of contrition of the penitent. Were the penitent not truly contrite, or in his confession used words he did not mean, he certainly would not be absolved, but would be committing, then and there, a new and perhaps greater mortal sin than any he had confessed.

"But how can the priest surely know that the penitent *is* sincere?" asks the sceptic. The answer to that is simple. The priest, who is a "mere man," cannot positively know whether the penitent is lying or telling the truth, but it is certain that God knows.

However, it would be a strange sort of Catholic who would go to confession with no good intention, or not at least meaning, "according to his lights," to be contrite. The one place that sort of person would avoid would be the confessional box; and the one person he would keep away from would be the priest.

Catholics do not go to confession to get away with anything. They well know they cannot. They go for but one purpose—to make their peace with the God Whom they know they have offended, and with the prayer that sanctifying grace may again be restored or increased in their souls. They know that God's mercy is infinite for all who penitently turn to Him in true humility.

5.

It remains to say a few words about the fancy that through the habit of confessing one's sins to a priest, he gets a "strangle hold" on you. This is the most grotesque of all the comical notions afloat in relation to the Sacrament of Penance. It is a piece with the silly statement often made, that priests charge a fee for hearing confessions. The latter absurd notion recalls a well-known story which has been many times repeated. A bitterly anti-Catholic Britisher, traveling in Belgium, poked his head into the vestibule of a Catholic church in Brussels and noticed a bulletin giving the hours of Mass—6, 7, 8, 9 o'clock and so on. As he could read no French or Flemish, he jumped to the conclusion that these figures were the prices charged by the priests for hearing confessions and forgiving sins, the amount of charge presumably governed by the seriousness of the sins confessed. And with this "proof" of his contention that Catholics had to pay cash for getting rid of their sins, he triumphantly returned home to spread the news among his Protestant friends!

But as to the "strangle hold." One very warm August afternoon some years ago, standing in line in St. Patrick's Cathedral at a confessional box, at least thirty people were ahead of me. More than an hour went by before my turn came to enter the box. And when I came out at least thirty more had arrived and were awaiting their turn.

No one would envy that hard-working priest, sitting in that stuffy box with the perspiration rolling down his face, and obliged to listen to and talk with perhaps a hundred or more men, women and children on the other side of the grille; giving each of them some advice and counsel, imparting absolution—if they deserve it—and then giving each a penance to perform and sending them all away with his blessing. And yet not knowing the identity of a single one of the hundred or more penitents.

Where does the "strangle hold" come in in that procedure? I'll tell you where it comes in. There are always many penitents who must bore priests to distraction with their trivialities and tiresome verbiage. He cannot know who they are unless they voluntarily disclose their identity; but he must patiently listen to them, whoever or whatever they are. He is always at their mercy; he cannot shake them off, even if tempted to do so. That is where the "strangle hold" comes in. The "strangle hold" is on the priest, not on the penitent.

Chapter Nine

THE CATHOLIC IDEA OF HUMOR

I.

"YOU CATHOLICS must lead a sad sort of existence, what with all your rules and regulations; your strict discipline, which requires you to go to Mass, willy-nilly, on Sundays; to eat fish on Friday, whether you like it or not; to check yourself up with a priest when you think you have broken a rule; to stop and think twice when you are tempted to have a little fun; to hesitate to read a book when you suspect it is off color; to fight shy of plays or movies if they have been put on the blacklist by your censor. And so on and so on. Why, man, you are so circumscribed by your Church that your whole life, if you do conform to the rules, must be a very bleak affair indeed. Even normal humor is taboo. You can't listen to funny stories with relish, if they happen to be a little spicy. And what is there to any funny story unless there is something spicy about it? Yes, you 'good' Catholics are a tragic bunch of people. I certainly pity you!"

Thus commented a rather vulgar but eminently rated business man, when one day he suspected that I was disgusted with his elaboration of a particularly filthy yarn he had been trying to regale me with. Not that ordinary sewerage shocks me; I've lived too long in this sordid world to be surprised or shocked by anything that exudes from the mouths of the average rough-house pagan. But this story was, after all, a bit too odoriferous, even though I was quite prepared for it. This person was of the vintage so vividly depicted by Father Leonard Feeney in one of his chapters in *You'd Better Come Quietly* [1]—the expansive Mr. Pig-face, who frankly, brutally and realistically spoils your dinner by spicing it with his vulgarisms.

All Catholics who appear to the outside public to be con-forming to the Catholic way of life, know that they are often pitied as unhappily circumscribed people who are not allowed any scope for the exercise of humor. But they usually indulge in a quiet smile when they hear this sort of pity expressed. For if there is one outstanding fact about Catholic life, it is that it is as redolent of humor as it is of joy. Catholics are the one class of humans who can carry along their sense of humor with their sense of reality. In-stead of proscribing or limiting humor in their daily lives, the Catholic way of life opens up avenues for indulgence in uproarious humor at times, which in no other circles of society could possibly exist.

Not that all individual Catholics are blessed with a high sense of humor; we do occasionally meet a painfully hu-morless Catholic. But he is quite surely a misfit. If you will trace his pedigree back far enough you are likely to find that somewhere in his ancestry there is a dour Scot or two —like John Knox, for instance. Anyhow, he is never an Irishman.

Catholic discipline, which my companion condemned so sweepingly, has no effect on the Catholic's sense of humor except to set it free and make it grow. This discipline aids

[1] *You'd Better Come Quietly*, by Leonard Feeney, Sheed & Ward, New York, 1940.

one to acquire a clear and vivid sense of relative values; to pick the wheat from the chaff; to know what is to the point and whether or not it is worth laughing over or crying over. One comes to see the world of men with clear eyes and as it really is; and he thus awakens to its humorous phases in many new and unusual ways.

First of all, in the domain of the Catholic's joy in his way of life, he learns to do one thing which many outside seem never to learn at all. He learns to suffer fools gladly. Since being in the Church, my own *penchant* for laughing has become far more pronounced than when, in the old days, I took seriously so many pointless things. I seldom if ever laughed at Catholics—individual Catholics—in those days. I just pitied them, like the critic just quoted. But nowadays I can understand all their idiosyncrasies and greet them all with a smile; and can laugh at, rather than pity, non-Catholics for their idiosyncrasies. I can even laugh at my own absurdities.

When first in the Church I was, perhaps, something of an amateur in all this, being, as I recall, slightly shocked when a jovial priest remarked to me one day:

"After you have been in the Church a while and get over taking yourself so seriously, with your solemn habit of attempting to discuss theology with every Catholic or non-Catholic you meet, you will give way to more than one good laugh at yourself. For by that time you will have realized what sort of eggs most of us are—and what sort you are yourself."

Of course the secret of that attitude is humility; the ability to appraise oneself and all others properly. That ability comes with Catholic experience and discipline. And with it comes the faculty of suffering gladly, not only the fools one finds within the fold, but those outside also. One can now view all absurdities without venom or hate, but in a kindly, sympathetic and charitable spirit. To be able to do this tempers many a trying situation, and surely adds to the joy of life. In fact it demonstrates anew the old adage that "it is fun to be a Catholic."

2.

Having done my best on these few pages to emphasize the joyfulness of living the Catholic life, despite its rules, regulations and discipline, it is now my intention to tell of a few incidents of my own experience which surely confirm the claim that opportunities for indulging in a smile do crop out in the daily life of the Catholic. Not that these incidents will seem amusing to those readers who take themselves too seriously; certainly not to the humorless, knitted brow type, the sort who readily believe that the moon is made of green cheese and that George Bernard Shaw is an authority on Catholic Christianity. Perhaps the devotees of Mr. Pigface's type of humor will think them dull and boresome. But this book is not written for such; it is written for the man in the street who is bored to death by the sordid views of life most of our popular pundits teach. He, at least, will see something amusing in the portrayals of people of the types he knows—and catch the moral too.

The first incident relates to the sort of person one often meets with nowadays—a Buchmanite. These Buchmanites, or Oxford Groupers, are also sometimes called First Century Christians. The latter, I believe, is their definitive title. They are not to be confused, however—as sometimes happens—with the Oxford Movement of a century ago in the

Church of England; they have no connection with that. They are a non-sectarian religious group, started some quarter century ago by Dr. Frank Buchman, a former Lutheran minister, who broke away from institutional Christianity, evidently influenced by the idea that churches, priesthoods, sacraments and dogmas are mere accretions of the pure gospel of Christ and should be done away with.

When you become a Buchmanite, you do not join a church; you simply ally yourself with the Group—whose gatherings have sometimes been called "house parties." When joining, however, you make your confession of faith; and you are permitted to confess your sins openly before all others in your group. Then it is expected that you will go forth to convert sinners. There are no regular Sunday services, no churches, and you may, even though a member, remain attached to any Christian church you wish. Everybody is welcome, regardless of other affiliations.

Now it happened that on a bitterly cold January morning in 1936, I started out from New York City to drive to Washington, en route to Florida, making the journey alone. The roads were more or less icy and while crossing New Jersey a heavy snowfall set in. After reaching the Delaware bridge at Lambertville and turning south on the road to Baltimore, it began to be very hard going. The windshield was caked with ice and snow. Chilled to the bone, I still kept on, hoping the temperature would rise farther south, and the snow turn to rain. But the farther south I got the colder it became and the heavier fell the snow.

Creeping along at no greater pace than twenty miles an hour, I finally got through the city of Norristown; and just south of that city, while picking my way on a slippery road through the ever-increasing snowfall, a tall man in a long black coat, his hat brim pulled down and his coat collar turned up so that it all but concealed his face, hailed me from the side of the road. At his side, resting on the snow, was a large black valise.

Seldom caring to pick up hitch-hikers (having learned my lesson in that regard) I was about to ignore this man when the thought flashed through my mind that he might be a priest. In this blinding snow, he could easily be taken for one. There was the black coat and black hat and also the black bag—large enough to contain a Mass kit. Deciding to risk it I slowed down and stopped. As he barged out to me, dragging his big valise through the snow, he exclaimed:

"Thank God for you! I've been praying for your arrival for the past hour. You *are* the Good Samaritan!" He lifted his hat and shook me warmly by the hand.

The face—now that I could see it—proved that he was no priest. They never look like that—nor do they ever ask a stranger such a question as he at once propounded. As soon as he was comfortably seated and we had started on, he turned to me with a solemn earnest look and asked:

"May I put to you a personal question?—Have you made your peace with God?"

You think I had taken aboard an escaped lunatic? Not at all. An Oxford Grouper was on my hands; a "First Century Christian." Having met such before, there was no room for doubt. To his question I quietly replied:

"At least I hope so. I try to be a good Catholic."

"CATHOLIC?" he exclaimed, shifting to the outer edge of the seat, as though he feared I might bite. "Why—why— you don't look like a *Catholic*. You look for all the world like a Protestant."

"Sorry, but I'm a Catholic just the same. What is your faith, may I ask? Christian of any sort?"

"Yes, indeed, I'm a Christian. Not a member of any sect, though brought up a Lutheran. I'm now one of Dr. Buchman's Group—you've no doubt heard of that. First Century Christians, you know."

"That's interesting," I observed. "I'm a first century Christian myself."

"I thought you said you were a Catholic?"

"I did. But in the first century all Christians were Catholics. You must know that. And the Catholics of today are the same as those of the first century after Christ. They still believe and teach the same things they did then. They have been doing just that for nineteen centuries."

"Are you sure of that?" he earnestly asked. "Why, didn't St. Patrick start the Catholic Church? The Irish are all Catholics. Are you Irish—or Irish descent? I wouldn't guess so. That's why I said you look like a Protestant, not a Catholic."

"Does a Catholic have to look like an Irishman—or be an Irishman? What about Italians, Frenchmen, Spanish, German, Polish—and pure Americans too. There are a lot of English Catholics also—even some Scotch Catholics. And I know some Jews who are Catholics."

You may say it is extraordinary that anyone, not a pure moron, would assume that the Catholic Church was founded by St. Patrick. But do we not too often overlook the fact that millions of supposedly educated Americans know but the merest smattering of history prior to the discovery of America? In public school in my day I was never taught any history except that of the United States and the Colonies. Many Americans no doubt go through life

assuming that Christopher Columbus antedated Julius Caesar, that Alexander the Great and Peter the Great were
contemporaries, and so on. Some years ago I knew a member of Congress who asked me this innocent question:
"Weren't Julius Caesar and Caesar Borgia one and the same
person?" That man, before going to Congress, had long
been a member of the Board of Education in his own home
town!

When it comes to the history of Christianity, ignorance
is still more dense. A devout Methodist youth (who had a
common school education) once insisted to me that John
Wesley had lived "around the time of the Apostles," and
that the latter were all Methodists without any doubt. And
it was only a few years ago that a woman to whom I was
telling something about St. Francis of Assisi, and had explained that the worldwide Franciscan Order grew out of
his activities in the thirteenth century, made this naïve remark: "Oh yes, I've heard of the Franciscans. They are
what you call Jesuits, aren't they?" Perhaps the climax of
ignorance came to my notice when an American of some
culture and education asked me why the Pope wouldn't
allow the Catholics in Rome, Italy, to have a bishop!

But to return to my Buchmanite friend. My remark that
others besides Irish were Catholics, failed to click. My suggestion about the universality of Catholicism seemed to
make no impression. He went right on: "Well, didn't St.
Patrick convert the Irish to Christianity? And so didn't he
start the Catholic Church right there?"

Here I slipped in a laugh; but my companion was too
intensely serious to see anything to laugh at. "There is an
old story," he resumed, "about St. Patrick having driven
all the snakes out of Ireland. And an Irishman once told

me that Irish Catholics call Irish Protestants snakes in the grass. So I suppose when it is said that St. Patrick drove the snakes out, it really means that he drove the Protestants out, doesn't it?"

"Nothing in that," I said. "St. Patrick lived in the fifth century. There were no Protestants until the sixteenth century—so he couldn't have driven any out."

"Oh, you must be wrong about there being no Protestants until the sixteenth century. The First Century Christians were Protestants. We all know that. Why, even today Protestants name their churches and cathedrals after the great apostles. Look at that big Protestant cathedral in New York—St. John the Divine. Even the Methodists and Presbyterians call their churches after the apostles—St. James, St. Paul, and so on. The apostles *must* have been Protestants. Anyhow, we do know that St. Paul was a Protestant. I was taught that by my father, who was a Lutheran; he used to quote the great Martin Luther. St. Paul quarrelled with St. Peter; defied him to his face. Maybe Peter was a Catholic, but not St. Paul. We First Century Christians greatly admire St. Paul, for he certainly was one of us."

"St. Paul was a first century Christian," I agreed. "But a first century *Catholic*, not Protestant, Christian. Martin Luther, who started Protestantism, was a sixteenth century heretical Christian. St. Paul was a convert to Christ, not to Luther. He was the first great Catholic convert. And it was he who, in a sense, converted me."

That brought on a short meditation by my disputant. For a moment I thought he was stalled, but he soon broke out again.

"Oh, I see! That explains everything. You are a convert —you are *not* Irish! Have you been a convert for long?

I've heard of some emotional *young* people being converted to the Catholic religion; but as for mature men who have lived and learned—well, that *is* unusual."

"I imagine you haven't been an Oxford Grouper many years either," I said. "You must be in your fifties, at least. I've heard of some emotional *young* people being converted to Dr. Buchman's brand of religion, but as for mature men who have lived and learned—that is unusual."

He missed that one, and with great seriousness continued. "I changed because I wanted to get back to the Christianity of the first century; the true Christianity, without doctrines and dogmas, without Popes and priests; without churches and sacraments; without——"

Just then my car all but slid into the ditch. The big valise on the back seat crashed to the floor and the Grouper grew rigid with fright. "I hope you are saying a prayer," I exclaimed, as I worked the car back to the road. "It's very dangerous. If you would rather get out, it's all right with me." But I couldn't shake him; he wanted to go to Washington and this was his only chance to get there.

In response to his assertion that he wanted to get back to the vacuous Christianity he had pictured as existing in the first century, I indulged in a little more levity by paraphrasing him in the same way as before.

"I changed to the Catholic religion because I wanted to get back to the Christianity of the first century; the true Christianity, *with* its doctrines and dogmas, *with* its Popes and priests; *with* its churches and sacraments"—and so on. But he missed that too.

All along that endless Bel-Air road, through the network of Baltimore streets and on to Washington, he kept up a steady stream of pious piffle, boring me to distraction; I all but wished for a flat to break the monotony. At last, when we reached Washington well after nightfall, where I dropped him off with a great sigh of relief, he again shook me warmly by the hand, and said,

"I am full of gratitude and will never forget you as the Good Samaritan. And I am glad to have met such a fine member of the great Church that St. Patrick put on the map. . . ."

Now that isn't just a tall story. It actually happened. I have reproduced the verbiage as accurately as I can now recall it. Nor have I told the tale to cast ridicule on the Groupers, who are certainly sincere, have done a lot of good in some quarters, and who no doubt count many intelligent, if occasionally humorless, men and women amongst their following. This obviously sincere and in many ways appealing personality, though painfully ignorant, was perhaps no more typical of Buchmanism, than of any other groups who are profoundly ignorant of Catholic Christianity.

Anyhow, the foregoing story illustrates the sort of opportunity for indulgence in humor which often comes to the observing Catholic. I admit, however, that some non-Catholics might not view it as amusing. That's because they are without the Catholic point of view.

3.

In my second sample of the Catholic idea of humor, I am going to return to Wall Street—my real stamping ground.

There used to be in the financial district an allegedly wise, old arm-chair philosopher, who prided himself on his wide knowledge and great wisdom, as well as his acumen on the stock market. He was ready at all times to speak with authority on any subject under the sun—science, politics, economics, finance, the fine arts, or religion. Perhaps he did have a smattering of knowledge beyond the capacity of the ordinary man in the street. In any event, many there were who hung on his words of wisdom.

One day I was a guest of this seasoned old free-thinker and stock-market wizard, at a luncheon of half a dozen business men, among whom there happened to be one Catholic. It was before I had become a Catholic myself. The luncheon was on a Friday, but this meant nothing to our host, who had ordered luscious English mutton chops for all his guests. The Catholic, however, declined the chops, and to the evident embarrassment of the apologizing host, asked for some fish instead. And then, as it happened, the Catholic had to leave before the luncheon was quite over. Our host now took the floor on the subject of Catholicism. None of the others knew much about it, but he, of course, claimed to speak with authority.

"Oh, I knew he was a Catholic," he said, "but for a moment I had forgotten. No doubt he's sincere in it, although a bit daffy, of course. I've talked with him about it more than once. He is not a fool; he does seem to know all the strong arguments for Catholicism from the ground up. Of course there are real arguments for the Catholic view—provided you accept the basic ones."

"What basic ones?" asked several men in chorus.

"Well, you must believe in the existence of God for one thing. And you must believe that Jesus Christ was born of a Virgin, that He rose from the dead after being crucified, walked around in Palestine and talked, ate and slept like any of us, for forty days more; that He founded a Church and picked Peter—the most unreliable of his disciples except Judas—to head His Church. And then disappeared into heaven."

"But aren't those just fables?" asked a simple little broker. "I understand those ideas were exploded long ago."

"Oh, but the Catholics claim there is plenty of proof for all these things. And the Catholics do have arguments. Just get into a discussion with a Jesuit, as I once did, and he'll stand you on your head in no time. These Catholics are very logical, and if logic were an infallible guide, we would all have to become Catholics. But fortunately for you and me, logic is a very unsafe guide; you never know where it is leading you. Just try it on the stock market, and see where you come out. Logic is a good thing up to a point, but one should never be *too* logical. There is no question in my mind that the weakness of our Catholic friend who just left us, is that he is entirely too logical."

"Can't you convince him of that? Why don't you show him? Have you tried to?" This from the little broker.

"I've discussed things with him more than once; but he is, as I said, a bit daffy on the subject. So live and let live, I say. Of course, you all know my own view on these religious panaceas. All free-thinking Christians nowadays view God as merely the mystery back of life which we know nothing about. You ought to read a bit of old David Hume—or that modern chap, Russell—or wise old John Dewey up at Columbia. These boys show clearly enough that it's folly to try to unravel the mystery back of life. All we really know is that we men are just animals—like horses; we breed, we live, we die, without knowing what it's all about. And as for the idea Catholics hold, that Jesus

Christ was a God-man, those are just words. If God is only an idea, a view—a figment of the imagination—how could there be a God-man?"

"Maybe the Jesuit can tell you," ventured the simple little broker. Our fountain of wisdom ignored that, but some of us asked him to explain, if one did accept these basic Catholic beliefs, why other Catholic claims would logically follow; for instance, infallible Church, infallible Pope, and so on.

"Why, don't you see," replied the oracle, "the Catholics say that Christ was God Incarnate. If you assume the truth of that, then He was certainly infallible, and whatever He taught, whether it makes sense to you and me or not, must be true. And if, as an infallible God, He did found a Church on this earth and promised to protect that Church from error in teaching faith and morals, then the teachings of that Church *must* necessarily be infallibly true. All that's logical enough, isn't it? So you see where sticking to logic brings you out. It's absurd; dangerous. Don't ever dare to be too logical."

"Humph! But how about the doctrine of hell?" asked the broker. "Catholics still believe in that, I'm told. How can anyone of intelligence believe there's a hell? *That's* not logical at all. I've heard many a preacher say from the pulpit——"

"It *is* logical!" roared the oracle. " 'Logical as hell'—you've heard that phrase. If you stick to logic right through you *must* believe in hell—that is, if you believe in a God of justice to start with. If there were such a God as Catholics claim there is, He could not be a God of justice if He rewards everybody alike, good or bad, and provides no retribution for the wicked. If heaven is awaiting us all, and

we are all certain to go there, then all unrepentant sinners
—murderers, adulterers, thieves, criminals and all other
crooks, even Wall Street crooks—will be ultimately sure
of eternal bliss, won't they? They will finally wind up just
like the saints. If that's so, why should anyone try to be a
saint? Why not just have a high old time while we are here?
That's logical, isn't it?"

"Do *you* believe in hell, then?" nervously asked the
little broker. "I always assumed that you——"

"No, no; don't get me wrong; I'm just giving you the
Catholic view. As for myself, I don't believe in human immortality at all. Of course, it is logical to think there is some
purpose back of human life aside from living on this earth
fifty or sixty years or more, and then being blotted out
forever—just like a horse. But I say it's too damned logical
to solve the riddle of life in that easy way. Never let logic
carry you into that wishful fancy. Leave off logic at the
proper point and fall back on common sense. And it's common sense to believe that when we die that is the end—just
as it is with a horse. All else is just pie in the sky; there's no
doubt about it."

That was a genuine jolt for the simple little broker, who
really considered himself a Christian of a sort. "You don't
mean to say," he exclaimed, "that we flicker out for good?
That *is* a sockdologer to me. If that's so, then why call ourselves Christians at all—even 'liberal' Christians? What's
all the shooting for, if there's nothing to shoot at?"

So far as I can recollect, there was no answer to that from
the wise old oracle. He glanced at the little broker rather
disdainfully, as though he considered it a waste of time to
talk further with a moron, and then changed the subject.

I have often wondered if that atheistic harangue made

any impression on this group. It rolled off me like water on a duck's back, even though I was not then a Catholic. But I did learn long after how greatly it had upset the little broker. Some years after I had entered the Church, he one day said to me: .

"I surely envy you being so sure of things. Do you recall the talk at that luncheon when his windy old nibs sprang his sockdologers on religion—no God, no immortality, no hell and so on? I've often thought about it. Of course he didn't convince me any more than he convinced you. I still believe in God and I still believe in human immortality. . . . But there's the question of hell. He claimed that if there were a heaven there would have to be a hell, too. I don't believe there is such a thing as hell. But then, the trouble is, I don't surely know that. That's what sometimes frightens me. Isn't it HELL how little we do know?"

4.

You may not realize it, but it is a fact that some people in Wall Street (as well as many elsewhere) have the fancy that most Catholics in business circles strive to keep secret the fact that they are Catholics. There *is* a basis for this notion, even though a slight one. Such so-called Catholics do exist. To illustrate. Talking with a business man whom I understood was a Catholic—although he had never mentioned the fact to me—I made the casual remark that I had been down to Augusta, Georgia, the week before, where I had made a little address at the annual convention of the Catholic Laymen's Association. In obvious surprise he glanced up at me and exclaimed:

"What—you a Catholic? You surprise me; I never would

have dreamed it." Then, looking around the room where we were sitting (to be sure there were no eavesdroppers), he grew confidential, lowered his voice and said:

"Perhaps you don't know that I am a Catholic myself. But, like you, I try to keep it dark around here. Business reasons, of course." And then he immediately assured me he would be very careful to guard my own secret.

Wasn't that considerate of him—with me shouting it out from the housetops all the time!

These cryptic Catholics have always been a puzzle to me. How can one be a true Catholic if he has no more courage than that? A man once asked me if it would be possible for him to join the Church secretly—that is, keep it a permanent secret from his family and friends. Of course he no doubt *could* do that; but what an unhappy Catholic he would be! And I would be inclined to be sceptical about his sincerity. This thought has more than once come forcibly to my mind when some rumor is circulated regarding the alleged conversion of some person of prominence who seems to be toying with Catholicism or smiling at it receptively, but fears to make the plunge because of the attitude of a rich aunt or uncle.

Yet while I, for one, have never hesitated to proclaim my faith on every possible occasion in Wall Street or elsewhere, it seems to be a fact that news of this sort travels far more slowly among non-Catholics in Wall Street than do tips on the stock market, or rumors of prosperity or disaster just around the corner. I still occasionally meet some banker or broker known to me for years, who continues to rate me as a Protestant or pagan, and would, if told I am now a Catholic, declare it a libelous statement.

An incident of that kind occurred only a year or two

ago. A very honest, upstanding pious old banker, a devout practicing Protestant of the old Calvinistic school, took me aside one afternoon when I happened to drop into his office on business, and said:

"You are just the man I want to talk to. You have an enemy. I was recently told that you had become a Roman Catholic. What do you think of that sort of lie? Outrageous mud-slinging, I would call it. Of course I at once contradicted him. But I am sure you ought to know what some people are saying about you. Isn't gossip a vicious thing?"

"But I *am* a Catholic. Didn't you know that? Why, I've been a Catholic now for a good many years."

The old gentleman's jaw dropped and a look of unutterable sorrow overspread his features. For several moments he could not speak. Finally, in a sepulchral tone he asked:

"How in the world could a thing like that happen to you, of all men? And do you accept all the—the—superstitions? Or perhaps (his face lighting up a bit), perhaps you are one of the *liberal* Catholics—the kind who rise above the superstitions? I am sure you must be."

"What superstitions do you refer to?" I asked.

"Well, for instance; that thing they call the Mass. You surely cannot believe in a superstition like that? And then there are the images Catholics worship. Ignorant Catholics, I am told, actually kneel down before these graven images and pray to them. Why, they even pray to a string of beads they carry around in their pockets. I saw a nun on a train doing this once; an intelligent-*looking* nun. But she couldn't have been intelligent, actually. Oh, I'm not going on hearsay. But of course I know you are not that kind of Catholic; you surely must be one of the liberal sort who do not stoop to these silly superstitions."

Just to shock the old gentleman a bit I here took my own rosary out of my pocket. It was a very nice one; a gift from a friend. Dangling it before him I said:

"You see, I *am* that kind of Catholic. I am never without these prayer beads; they help me to say at least fifty prayers a day. Do you say fifty prayers a day? You are a good Christian, I know that. But as for me, I would find it hard to pray regularly and systematically without this aid; I would get careless."

"Humph! That's what I criticise about Catholics," he exclaimed, quite nettled. "They are always on their knees, praying. Praying to images—saints. Why don't they pray to God? Anyway, Christianity isn't just praying; it's living. My prayer is my good life."

"Fine," said I. "You are a good Catholic—if you mean that; if what you say is true. You are in the soul of the Catholic Church."

"*Me* in the Catholic Church? Not if I know it! What—what—do you mean?"

"I just mean," I explained, "that the Catholic Church recognizes good will and good faith in everyone who possesses those traits, even though they may be invincibly ignorant of Catholic truth. All such well intentioned people are said to be in the 'soul' of the Church. And certainly, if your life is as good as you imply, you must be included."

"Nonsense, nonsense; I won't have it!" The dear old gentleman was getting irascible. "Is that what they call Jesuitical casuistry? And do you think—do you think that I—*I*—should worship images?"

"No; nor Catholics either. No Catholic worships an image. What you call 'images' are merely statues—some of them very crude I'll admit—which are simply reminders of the particular saint to which the Catholic wishes to pray; just as the Figure on the Cross pictures to us, and reminds us, of Christ's suffering on the cross. Catholics appeal to the saints in heaven, not to their 'images' on earth."

"Humph! All this praying to saints is superstition. I believe in prayer; but prayer should be directed to God. That's what we do in my church."

"So do we. But we also petition the saints to pray for us, knowing that they can and will do so. And especially do we believe that the Queen of Saints, the Blessed Mother of Christ, will pray for us if we petition her rightly. We don't 'worship' the saints in the sense that we worship God. They are all creatures like ourselves, and our appeal to them is like an appeal you might make to a friend or to me, if you were in a dire situation and thought our prayers might help. You would not hesitate to ask a friend to pray for you under such circumstances? Haven't you often said to someone who was about to go to church, 'Do say a prayer for me'?"

"But saints are *dead*. I would only ask *living* persons to pray for me. To pray to a dead saint, it seems to me, is just like praying to a dead stone image."

"That's an odd idea," I commented. "You must excuse me; I thought you believed in human immortality?" I hated to say it to the kindly old man at that.

A blank stare, a startled look followed. And then the dear old gentleman, his belligerency fading away, said very gently, "Perhaps there *is* something in what you say, though I never thought it through. Yes, Paul the great Apostle *must be* alive in heaven, of course." He raised his eyes to the ceiling, thinking.

And then, dropping the subject of saints, he reverted to

the "superstition" of the Mass. Surely, I didn't take that seriously? When I undertook to briefly explain the meaning of the Mass, and said that no one can be a Catholic without believing in it; that all Catholics who practice their faith go to Mass every Sunday, he immediately demurred.

"Oh, I certainly question that statement," he said. "I have a number of Catholic neighbors, and while they may be good people they seldom if ever go to church on Sunday. Many times, when going to my own church Sunday morning, I've seen them starting out for the golf course."

"Probably they had already been to Mass. Many Catholics go to Mass before breakfast every Sunday."

"What? And then deliberately desecrate the Sabbath by playing golf all day? Would you call *that* the practice of Christianity?"

"Most decidedly. I have seen priests and even bishops sometimes playing golf Sunday afternoon. That is not 'desecrating' the Sabbath; that is harmless recreation, just as your work on cross-word puzzles Sunday afternoon is harmless recreation. Don't you call it practicing Christianity to go to church on Sunday morning at seven or eight o'clock, instead of lolling in bed and then enjoying a bountiful breakfast before giving any thought to God on His own Holy Day?"

That seemed to hit the bull's eye, for the discussion now ended with smiles on both sides. "Well, let's call it a day," he said. And we switched the conversation to the money market.

CHAPTER TEN

THE MAKING OF SAINTS

I.

THE COMMUNION OF SAINTS! As is the case with many people who know little or nothing about the beautiful doctrine of the Communion of Saints, the term had but the vaguest meaning for me during the long stretch of years preceding my Catholic life. Although brought up in a Christian family and taught from childhood to recite the Apostles' Creed with its phrase, "I believe in the Communion of Saints," I could not, to save my soul, have given an intelligible explanation of what the phrase meant. No one, either in or out of church, had ever explained it clearly to me.

But the Catholic Church did explain it. I now learned for the first time that the Communion of Saints is the spiritual solidarity which binds together the faithful on earth, the souls in Purgatory and the saints in Heaven, "in the organic unity of the Mystical Body of Christ"; and that all the living, including those who may not belong to the Visible Church on earth, share in this communion according to the measure of their union with Christ and with the soul of the Church.

In Catholic teaching, therefore, saints are not limited to those who are canonized, nor even to those who are members of the Visible Church on earth. The Church recognizes sainthood wherever it exists among men of good will who are in good faith. All such are in the soul of the Church, whether they are themselves aware of that fact or not.

Aside from this, however, the word "saints" has many other connotations among men. It is often used as a designation for any good, right-living person. In a more restricted sense also, as among Protestant Christians, the saints are the Twelve Apostles and the leading evangelists of Apostolic times, though often a few of the early Fathers of the Church are included in this category. And then we have that class who verbally "canonize" certain distinctly Catholic saints of the ages—St. Jerome, St. Augustine, St. Francis of Assisi, and so on. In the Anglican Church certain early British Catholics receive recognition as saints; for example, St. Anselm, St. Edward the Martyr, St. Dunstan, St. Thomas à Becket. Perhaps the broadest use of the word "saint" is found among our friends, the Mormons, who call their church, "The Church of Jesus Christ of Latter Day Saints." Every practicing Mormon, male or female, is a "saint"; just as every male Mormon from his fourteenth year on, is a member of the Mormon "priesthood."

In modern times the word "saint" is used in both a complimentary and a disdainful way. Even those who are not Christians seldom hesitate to apply the term to those whose good lives they admire, and often grant it to certain characters in history whose lives seem good or heroic. On the other hand, the word "saint" is often applied in derision to pious persons or to those individuals who avoid vulgarity, or disdain to mix with the tin sports and roustabouts. "He's a decent chap, too decent; a bit of a saint," is the sort of compliment they sometimes get.

However, when we view Christian history throughout

its long nineteen centuries, we find that the only saints ever *officially* accorded that title are Catholic saints. No person has ever been pronounced a "saint" by any of the Protestant sects. Many of their leaders and founders are venerated as Godly men, but even the most outstanding of the Protestant reformers—Luther, Calvin, Cranmer, Zwingli or others equally prominent—are not called saints. One may agree that John Wesley, for instance, was a very saintly man; but we fail to find him honored as a saint, even by the church which grew out of his teachings.

In the Catholic Church, however, saints are legion. Canonized saints, both ancient and modern, are found in her vast galaxy, and new saints are being added to the roster all the time. For while the Catholic Church, throughout her long life, has been plentifully burdened with sinners—being made up, as she necessarily is, of weak and faltering humans—nevertheless her whole mission in this world is *to make saints.*

The pagan world, in its natural attitude of scepticism and incredulity, seldom misses an opportunity to proclaim that the Church has had her bad popes, and that in her long history more than one great sinner has succeeded, for a time, in being influential in some of her councils—facts which the Church herself deplores but never denies. But the further fact that such incidents have always been overcome, is usually ignored—even contradicted—by those who instinctively hate the Church. The Catholic Church has never been swayed from her true mission of making saints. Indeed it has often happened that more and greater saints have come to the surface during her times of laxity, or when the Church is being bitterly persecuted, than during more normal times. Whenever her enemies proclaim, as they have many times, that the Church is on her last legs and will soon pass out, she invariably astonishes the world by producing many great saints.

It is a startling fact that when we examine periods of great unsettlement in history; the breaking up of the Roman Empire, the centuries of chaos known as the Dark Ages, the confusion throughout Europe during the rise and fall of the feudal system; and finally the breaking asunder of Christendom in the sixteenth century—we find all these periods marked with the emergence of many great Catholic saints. One has only to think of such men as St. Jerome and St. Augustine, of St. Ambrose and St. Benedict; of the galaxy of great saints who arose in the twelfth and thirteenth centuries—St. Thomas Aquinas, St. Bonaventura, St. Dominic and St. Francis of Assisi; and finally of the many great leaders who appeared in the sixteenth and seventeenth centuries, when Christendom was seemingly falling apart, and when numerous non-believers foresaw the complete collapse of Catholicism—St. Ignatius Loyola, St. Francis Xavier, St. Charles Borromeo, St. Francis Borgia, St. Peter Canisius, St. Robert Bellamine—and a long list of others too numerous to mention.

2.

Much reflection on the significance of sainthood preoccupied me when, in the spring of 1937, my wife and I sailed through the Panama Canal, en route to California. We were on one of the Grace Line boats which touched at several Caribbean ports, one of these being the famous old town of Cartagena on the northerly South American coast —still a port of importance in the Republic of Colombia.

Originally settled by the Spaniards in the early sixteenth century, Cartagena was several times attacked and plundered by the pirates and buccaneers who roamed the southern seas in those days; one of these being the famous British buccaneer, Sir Francis Drake, who stormed and subdued the town in the year 1595, nearly fifty years after the Spaniards had first settled there. Later on, Cartagena became the chief American port for the African slave trade, thriving for many years on the barbarous industry of corralling Negroes in Africa, taking them across the Atlantic in chains, and selling them as slaves in the American markets.

Cartagena, however, has a fame more inspiring than that of a slave market. It was the home for many years of St. Peter Claver, a Jesuit missionary priest of education and culture, a Spaniard by birth, who apparently had a more apostolic conception of the priestly vocation than did some others of his time. After the completion of his education in Majorca, and probably against the wishes of his parents, who had planned for him a career in the priesthood at home —perhaps to the attainment of some important bishopric— he joined the Society of Jesus, and was sent as a missionary to Cartagena, where he was ordained to the priesthood in the year 1616, at the age of thirty-six.

In Cartagena Peter spent the remaining thirty-eight years of his life in the work of alleviating the sufferings, both corporal and spiritual, of the hordes of unfortunate blacks who were being brought in chains, year after year, from the African coast. In this nefarious business an average of a thousand Negroes were landed here every month. Even though half of this monthly cargo sometimes died on the voyage, the trade was immensely profitable. Neither the repeated censures of the Pope, nor those of many Catholic moralists, could prevail against this method of making easy money. Nor could the missionaries stop it. All they could do was to try to alleviate the sufferings of the victims; and the outstanding heroic worker in this field was Father Peter Claver.

Father Claver had been timid and diffident as a youth; but here he soon became a bold and ingenuous organizer and leader. To get the confidence of the Negroes when they arrived, he organized a group of interpreters of the various negro dialects, whom he also trained as catechists, and whose first duty was to impress upon the unfortunate and suffering victims that he was their friend and would be their defender. Each month, as the ships arrived, he made it a practice to go out in a small boat to meet the incoming ship, with food and medicines for the suffering blacks. This practice was powerful in winning their confidence, of course. The Negroes, packed in the hold of the ships, always arrived crazed with hunger, fear and suffering.

While these suffering victims were penned in at Cartagena until they could be sold, Father Peter instructed and baptized them, besides doing everything possible to relieve their sufferings and comfort them; as well as protect them in every possible way from the cruelties of their oppressors. He was often criticised by the well-to-do whites for giving the Sacraments to creatures "so low that they scarcely possessed a soul"; and protests were again and again lodged by these pharisees with his superiors in Spain.

Nevertheless, in the face of all such protests and humiliations, with a light heart, he went steadily on. If the support of men was lacking, the strength of God was with him. He became famous as the miracle worker of all New Granada, and before he died is said to have baptized, with his

co-workers and assistants, a fabulous number of negroes—
some have put the figure at 300,000. He died in 1654 at the
age of seventy-four. He was canonized by the Church in
1888. His fame still persists among the descendants of the
faithful who lived in Cartagena in his time. He is the patron
saint of them all. His body (enclosed in glass) still lies
under the high altar in the local cathedral, which bears his
name. Standing in the public square of the town, this cathedral is an impressive monument to his memory.

Cartagena is by all odds the hottest place I have ever been
in. It is cursed with humidity under a boiling sun most of
the time. "Next door to the fiery gates," was the way the
purser on the ship described it to me the night before we
arrived. Still, to approach the harbor by boat in the early
morning when the atmosphere is clearest, is really a worthwhile experience. The picturesque old town with its red
tiled roofs straggling up the hillside from the water's edge;
the beautiful harbor, dotted with small islands of curious
rock formation; the mountains rising out of the sea to both
east and west, with the great Andes range looming in the
distance to the south—all this is a panorama long to be
remembered.

Fortunate we were that we entered this beautiful harbor
in the early morning, just as the sun was rising and before
the mist and heat of the day had begun to pile up too heavily. As the ship was to remain in dock all day to unload and
reload freight, nearly all the passengers went ashore. All
wanted to see the old fortification ruins and other traces of
the days of wars and piracy. And no doubt many wished
to tour the town to see the other points of interest, to shop
for souvenirs, and to discover attractive luncheon places,
or cafés where cooling drinks were served.

My wife and I were of the few who were more interested in the traces of Peter Claver than in those of the days of pirates and buccaneers—though we naturally did wish to see all that as well. We had been reading on our way down from New York, Arnold Lunn's *A Saint in the Slave Trade*,[1] a short life of St. Peter Claver. This had whetted our interest in the heroic slave-trade saint. We went directly from the boat to the cathedral, where we saw his body still preserved under the high altar, and his quaint little chapel adjoining the cathedral. And we also saw the little wooden altar now in the chapel, which, we were told, he built with his own hands.

The cathedral is of that Spanish type of ecclesiastical architecture of centuries back, of rather ornate rococo style; it is in a good state of preservation although very musty, as all churches in such a humid climate are bound to be. We inspected the interior with a group of tourists who had followed us in; but they, not being Catholics, and apparently knowing nothing about St. Peter Claver, gave only the usual tourist glances, asked no questions, and soon hastened to return to the sun-baked square.

We, of course, lingered longer in this consecrated spot; and shortly several other Catholics came in. Naturally we were of these few who said a prayer or two and tried for a little while to commune in spirit with the heroic saint, who had lived and wrought here during those far distant days, three centuries ago. To meditate for a time in the place where Father Claver had given so many long years of his priestly life to bring the charity of Christ and the light of Christianity to those suffering black men, women and chil-

[1] *A Saint in the Slave Trade*, by Arnold Lunn, Sheed & Ward, New York, 1935.

dren, carrying on day after day, season after season, year after year, in that torrid climate—was indeed to glimpse more than the natural; it was to glimpse the supernatural.

There is an interesting oil painting of Father Claver in the small chapel. Whether it is a perfect likeness, or has been idealized by some artist, I do not know. In any event it shows a remarkable face, a happy face, with strong, handsome features, a gentle winning smile and large brilliant eyes which startle one, so deep and penetrating are they. The portrait reminded me of a picture of Father Junipero Serra, the famous founder of the California Indian missions in the eighteenth century, which hangs in one of the private dining rooms of Notre Dame University. Not that the features are in any way similar, but this portrait of Father Serra also shows amazingly glorious eyes; eyes which seem to penetrate to eternity.

That morning in the Cartagena chapel I lingered long before this portrait of Peter Claver; went back to it again and again. I wanted to return in the afternoon, but time would not permit. It was indeed the face of a saint; in memory it haunts me still.

3.

"What did you see in that hell-hole? Was it worth while going ashore in all that heat?"

Thus inquired one of the passengers that evening as we were getting underway again, en route for Colon and the Canal. This man had not gone ashore himself, being very much of an invalid; and in any event not at all interested in sight seeing. He was, as he had already confided to me, "a man of the world who had seen the world," and was utterly fed up on sightseeing of every kind. He said he was making this trip to California purely for his health.

I had already had several talks with this man of the world who had seen the world. Interesting enough he was, but an all too voluble talker. That very morning, as we stood on the deck at dawn, viewing the scene as the ship worked her way into the beautiful harbor, he had expressed himself in the following rhetorical flourish.

"When I view this resplendent scene; this natural harbor so curiously marked with these protruding rocks; these majestic mountains rising out of the great blue sea, and the great snow-capped range to the south;—when I see all this, I realize, and you must have the same thought, that as compared with great Mother Nature, we humans are the merest insects and of no importance at all. We are nothing but flies hovering about for our brief day, and then passing away as we came. But Mother Nature is always here. That great mountain rising out of the sea to our right, will never die; but you and I, perhaps twenty years hence, will have gone forever—dead as a doornail. We men, strutting around in our vanity, are *nothing* as compared with these majestic mountains!"

How often we hear that sort of nonsense—even from some people whom we assume are intelligent. Quite naturally I took my companion to task a bit. Said I, "Sometimes we do no thinking before breakfast. You are overlooking a few traits about human beings which you will never find in mountains or anywhere else in inanimate nature. You can see those mountains, but they cannot see you. You can talk and you can reason, you can walk or run; you can laugh or cry; you can love or hate. You can look in upon yourself and out upon the world. Nor are you a mere

robot or automaton; you can decide, and you can choose
your acts and movements. You have a free will to govern
your acts; you can acquire knowledge if you will, or remain
ignorant if you will. You can propagate your kind or not,
as you choose. Can mountains, can inanimate nature, do
any of these things?"

He looked startled, and then laughed. "That's a thought,"
was his comment as he left me to go down to breakfast.

In answer to his query as to whether it had been worth
while to go ashore in all the heat, I said:

"Perhaps it wasn't worth while for the ordinary sights;
it was boiling hot all day. But despite the heat, it was well
worth while to go to the cathedral and see the traces of the
slave-trade saint, Peter Claver."

"Peter Claver? Who was Peter Claver? Never heard of
him."

That question offered an opportunity to enlarge upon
the history and virtues of the saint, which I immediately
proceeded to do. Several other passengers stepped across
the deck to listen in. Not one of them had ever heard of
Peter Claver—yet they had all visited the cathedral as tourists that day. However, they now listened with keen interest, and asked many questions. But the man of the world
who had seen the world was not impressed; evidently he
didn't believe in saints. To him saints were merely un-
balanced fanatics. That must have been the case with Peter
Claver. To save the lives of negro slaves was too whimsical
for words. What good did it do? They remained slaves and
died slaves, so why try to prolong their lives? And as for
Peter Claver himself, his whole life must have been spent
in misery, without even a moment of happiness.

A comment by one of the more sympathetic listeners

was quite apropos here. She suggested that if this man of the world had himself been living at that period, he would no doubt have been a slave-trader himself. It was a dirty business, but there was big money in it. To his credit, however, the oracular one demurred.

Later that evening this man of the world unburdened himself to me on the problem of happiness and of life in general. There was no such thing in this world as happiness, he contended. At least he had never experienced it, despite a long and successful business and social career, with full opportunity to see the worthwhile things of the world. Passing pleasures he had certainly known; but no true happiness at any time.

In the course of that long evening, I tried to tell him something about the Catholic view of happiness; but it made little impression, so far as I could see. Finally we lapsed into silence, watching the moon in the eastern sky and the flickering stream of moonlight on the water. And then he remarked, as he arose to go in for the night:

"Well, it would be wonderful if life had a meaning; if your ideas of life were true. That, of course, would explain and justify Peter Claver."

I remained on deck for another half hour, watching the moonlight on the water and thinking of Peter Claver; thinking of that heroic slave-trade saint, for whom life *did* have a meaning, and who had found the happiness which this "man of the world who had seen the world" had never found in all his wanderings.

4.

"There were giants in the Church in those days," remarked a non-Catholic friend to me one day when we were

talking about St. Peter Claver, and also about another Jesuit
missionary of those times, St. Isaac Jogues.

"You Catholics," he continued, "have produced many
great saints, all the way from apostolic times to recent centuries. But one thing I have noticed; very few modern
saints seem to have been canonized in our time. Is it that in
modern life the art of sainthood is dying away? Most of
those canonized nowadays, it appears, are men and women
who lived long ago. For example, Sir Thomas More and
Bishop John Fisher, who were recently canonized, died
over four hundred years ago. Isn't it a fact then, that the
Catholic Church is not so prolific nowadays as in the past
in making saints?"

Of course it was a simple matter to name for my friend
a long list of saints who lived during the eighteenth and
nineteenth centuries, as well as a group of recently canonized saints, some of whom lived on until men still living can
remember some of them. Such great names as St. John
Viannay (Curé D'Ars), St. John Bosco, St. Theresa of
Lisieux (the Little Flower), and so on. All of these my
friend had overlooked, as well as several others still more
recently canonized.

A fact to emphasize, which many people overlook, is that
the test of sainthood is not canonization. That is simply
confirmation of the fact that, after thorough investigation,
it has been proven that the person concerned became a saint
during his or her life. Many years, even centuries, may
elapse, as in the case of St. Thomas More and of St. John
Fisher, before a particular saint is granted the grace of
canonization; but St. Thomas More and St. John Fisher
were already saints when they went to the block in 1535.
After that they were also martyrs. Peter Claver was a saint

before he died in 1654, although he was not formally canonized until 1888—more than two hundred years later. In this, our own time , many heroic saints known only to God are no doubt scattered throughout the world, some of whom may, long after this generation of men is gone, be formally recognized and canonized.

Undoubtedly there are living amongst us today large numbers of "saints in the making"; outstandingly good and heroic men and women whose way of life is forming them into saints. For after all, what *are* saints? A person is not a saint because of his possession of superior talents, cleverness or brilliancy of mind, or exceptional education. Voltaire, for instance, possessed such qualities as these, but even his greatest admirers would not call him saintly. Nor is it genius, such as one would see in Thomas A. Edison; nor statesmanship. We Americans venerate George Washington and Abraham Lincoln, but certainly not as saints.

Saints are, first of all—to quote St. Cyprian of long ago —"other Christs." They have succeeded in living a Christlike life. As Father Martindale put it so lucidly in his little book, *What Are Saints?*, "Amazing as may be the identity of mind and feeling that can come about between two human friends, or between man and woman truly and thoroughly in love with one another and lastingly so, this is as nothing to the 'interpenetration' of the saint's mind and Christ's mind; the unification of the saint's heart with Christ's Heart; the indwelling, in the saint, of Christ's own Spirit." [1]

Little as most of us know about each other, we often try to pick the wheat from the chaff. We say such and such a

[1] *What Are Saints?* by C. C. Martindale, S.J., Sheed & Ward, New York, 1940.

person is a saint, or at least living a saintly life. But we all too easily go astray in our judgments of others. We gladly praise someone whom we realize is better than we; just as we often condemn someone who may be far better than we. At times we may be right in our judgments, but perhaps far more often wrong.

Yet we may, if sufficiently observant and just, now and then detect, with reasonable accuracy, the decidedly saintly qualities displayed by some who are trying to live Christ-like lives. And I am going to try, in the next few pages, to illustrate this by briefly detailing one present-day manifestation of "sainthood in the making," which is, it seems to me, right before our eyes. It is of course only one manifestation of the true imitation of Christ in ways of living. The imitation of Christ is going on all around us, in all parts of the world, by heroic souls in many vocations. We unheroic people are often too blind to see the realities of heroic Christlike lives, as expressed perhaps at times, even by our next-door neighbors.

5.

Here is the illustration referred to above. One morning eight or nine years ago, the young woman whose duty it was to greet callers in my business office and ascertain their wishes, came in to me and, in a tremulous voice, exclaimed:

"There's a strange-looking man outside who says he wants to speak with you. But I don't think you should let him in. He looks too much like a Communist. Shall I shoo him away?"

"No, bring him right in," I said. "It would be a novelty to have a Communist in here."

A moment later a brawny, stocky man walked in; and at first glance I knew my slender little feminine watch-dog could never have shooed him away had he not chosen to go. He was muscular.

That is the way I came to meet Peter Maurin, co-worker with Dorothy Day, the editor of the *Catholic Worker*. Until then I had known little or nothing of Dorothy Day, beyond the fact that she was trying to carry on in the lower East Side of New York City, a lay Catholic charitable movement among the down-and-outs. I had never seen a copy of her paper; I really knew nothing more about her than that. But by the time Peter Maurin left me that morning, I knew a whole lot about her.

Anyone who has met Peter knows that he can, on first appearance, make the shivers creep up your spine when he begins to talk. If, when he starts in, you are leaning back in an easy chair, you will find yourself sitting erect in that chair before he has talked five minutes. He can cram more truth into your cranium at high speed in a single hour than any ordinary person could in a week. He doesn't talk *with* you, he talks *at* you—as though he were addressing a mass meeting. And that morning I was the mass meeting.

His theme was social justice. He gave me, among other things, the gist of Pope Pius XI's encyclical *Quadragesimo Anno*—which up to that time I had not digested at all. But Peter had digested it, and he made its contents so clear to me that a short time thereafter I was able to give a brief talk on it to a small group of high-brow Wall Streeters, and actually tell them some things they didn't already know.

When Peter had finished this long lecture on social justice, and allowed me to get in a few words edgeways, I timidly asked him to tell me something about Dorothy

Day's activities. At once he was off on another oration. He finally wound up with an earnest plea—in fact a demand—that I go up to Union Square some evening and confound the Communists with a militant speech in support of Catholic social justice.

Naturally I sidestepped that suggestion quite obliquely. Just picture me in Union Square, bucking the Communists and getting lost in the shuffle under ten feet of débris!

But through Peter I shortly thereafter met Dorothy Day. And then it was I learned that, down in the lower East Side, the charity of Christ was being objectively expressed in an altogether unique way to many of us comfortable people, who sit in arm chairs in Wall Street and really know very little at first hand about what is going on all around us to alleviate the sufferings of some of the most unfortunate and "down-trod" of God's children.

Now here, in this House of Hospitality movement of Dorothy Day's—which has spread all over the country since that time of my first insight into it—there can surely be had a glimpse of "sainthood in the making." It is a sad commentary that her principles and methods have been criticised or ridiculed—even by some Catholics. Said one critic to me several years ago, "They may mean all right, but they do such foolish things. They hand out food to or take in *anybody* for a night's lodging—even bums and panhandlers. They run their affairs not like sensible folk but like a lot of children."

Like a lot of children! Exactly. It is childlike because it is Christlike. Unless, as do little children, we recognize that all other children are God's children, I am afraid we never get very far in our understanding of the charity of Christ. And no one can understand Dorothy Day's House of Hospitality movement until he comes to see that it is the charity of Christ in action.

What is the charity of Christ? St. John the Apostle summed it up for us. "Whosoever hath the substance of this world and beholdeth his brother in need, and shutteth up his heart to him, how doth the love of God abide in him? Little children, let us not love with word, neither with the tongue, but in deed and in truth."

To love in deed and truth means, if it means anything, performing, insofar as we can, the seven corporal works of mercy, and also the seven spiritual works of mercy. The corporal works are: To feed the hungry, to give drink to the thirsty, to clothe the naked, to harbor the harborless, to visit the sick, to ransom the captive, and to bury the dead.

And the spiritual works of mercy—what are they? To instruct the ignorant, to counsel the doubtful, to admonish sinners, to bear wrongs patiently, to forgive offences willingly, to comfort the afflicted, to pray for the living and the dead.

The ordinary modern charitable movement, whether organized or unorganized, is usually primarily operated to perform the corporal works of mercy, and while undoubtedly an immense amount of good is done in this way, yet the corporal works are mainly works of mercy for the body; not so much for the soul. It is important that the corporal works be performed, but is it not equally important that we perform the spiritual works also? That, surely, was Christ's teaching. And these people who have been building up the House of Hospitality movement, are trying to perform the spiritual as well as the corporal works of mercy, insofar as they are able to do so with the wholly inadequate help they get from others.

It has been my fortunate privilege to get at least a slight glimpse of this House of Hospitality movement; and I know how genuine it is. Some people may wonder why this little Catholic group are so persistent in agitating for social justice; why they continuously quote the Papal labor encyclicals. Why are they always emphasizing the need for religious instruction, as well as the need for coffee and food and clothing for those they are trying to help? Why do they seem so interested in bringing a fallen-away Catholic back to the Sacraments, or any Christian or non-Christian back to God?

The answer to such questions is the same as was given the critics of St. Peter Claver three centuries ago. Why did he make it his paramount duty to baptize the negroes as well as nurse and feed them? Why did he try to lead them to the Sacraments as well as do all he could to relieve their physical sufferings? The answer to those questions is that he was trying to perform the spiritual as well as the corporal works of mercy.

And that is what Dorothy Day's group have been trying to do for the past ten years or more. How far they have been successful in this apostolic work is not so much the test as how consistently they have adhered to their intentions under heavy obstacles. But they *have* succeeded to a surprising degree. Criticised, laughed at, scorned by the smug and uncharitable—yes, of course. The same thing was true with Peter Claver. He also was criticised, hampered, scorned and humiliated, but he went happily and joyously on.

"All our fellow workers in our twenty-one branches throughout the country have pledged themselves to voluntary poverty and manual labor. They will take less so that others will have more. They are trying to reach the poverty of the stable in which Christ was born." Thus ran a statement in the *Catholic Worker* a few years ago. There are now not twenty-one but over forty Houses of Hospitality in this country, and the movement has even spread to other countries.

Surely we do not have to search back to past times to learn about "sainthood in the making." It is always before our eyes. Countless other instances in this country, also before our eyes and to be seen, if we will only look for them, are going on all around us; outstandingly, of course, among the religious Orders; but also among the laity. I think often of the work now being carried on at Fellowship House, by that remarkable Russian noblewoman, the Baroness Catherine de Hueck, who is bringing the charity of Christ to the needy in New York's colored colony—thus emulating St. Peter Claver in a very striking way. But I have enlarged upon the activities of Dorothy Day and her group, because, as in my visit to Cartagena I discovered St. Peter Claver, this House of Hospitality movement has also come before my eyes.

Chapter Eleven

LIFE'S ENRICHMENT

I.

AN exhaustive study of modern capitalism, as the creator of practically all the blessings to be found in civilized life as we know it today, made something of a stir recently, particularly among that class of business men and industrialists who are important factors in "turning the wheels of modern progress." [1] It was a brilliant presentation of the point of view of the modern materialistic mind. The writer of this portentous volume undertook to prove, partly by means of voluminous statistical studies and exhibits, that scientific progress, primarily in the field of mechanical invention, has brought untold blessings to the human race—blessings mainly due to the fact that modern capitalistic society has been broadly developed and all but perfected, as a result of the concentration of great aggregations of capital and credit in the hands of the master minds of our time. This is the key to the comfort and happiness of us all. And of course the author again and again deprecates the fact that this profound truth is not at all comprehended by the rank and file of present-day reformers.

In sum, he points out—and seems to prove—that modern life for all of us has been enormously enriched through

[1] *Capitalism the Creator,* by Carl Snyder, The Macmillan Company, New York, 1940.

mechanical inventions such as labor-saving machinery and mammoth producing apparatus, with the speeding up of production and distribution, the cutting out of wasteful activities in all fields of wealth production, and the consequent elimination of both time and space. As a result of all this, creature comforts by the score, unknown to even the most affluent a half century ago, are now the commonplaces of the lowliest. All men are therefore sharing in the blessings of this progressive age of capitalism, and are living on a civilized level of high degree, such as has never before been known in history.

It is really a defence of the old classical political economy of Adam Smith, John Stuart Mill and Jeremy Bentham: the gospel of the "Manchester school" brought down to date and adorned in modern dress. The book is dedicated "to the prescient mind of Adam Smith" and this seer's portrait forms the frontispiece. It will therefore be realized that the author has scant sympathy for the present-day brand of New Deal reformers and is quite sweepingly critical of movements inspired by the belief that our mechanistic civilization has many shortcomings which should be remedied. It takes one's mind back to the days when, about the opening of the present century and the decade before, the "radicals" were still, for the most part, Jeffersonian democrats, talked free trade and opposed the rising trend toward regulation of business and restrictions on the freedom of corporate enterprise. The Jeffersonian aphorism, "that government is best which governs least," still seemed at that time the shibboleth of radicalism; nowadays it is the shibboleth of conservatism, and is cried down by many present-day radicals as "economic royalism."

An engaging and gripping book for any thoughtful

person to mull over, and very convincing provided one accepts its fundamental postulate—the postulate with which the famous agnostic, Thomas H. Huxley, upset William E. Gladstone seventy years ago; the postulate implying that England's great liberal leader was not created by Almighty God but had merely evolved from the gorilla family. In short, one must be an atheist or agnostic to accept wholeheartedly the theme of this book.

For the latter type it should have a great appeal; its logic fits an atheistic mind like a glove. For scientific advance has indeed been the creator of this wonder age of ours. Modern mechanical inventions have so eliminated time and space, have supplied us with so many labor-saving devices and have taught us so many short cuts for reaching ends that, compared with the days of yore, we are living in a wholly different world, a never-never world, never dreamed of by our earlier poets and prophets. It is a world not dreamed of even fifty years ago.

When a youth in my twenties—which was fifty years ago—I could add a column of a million or more figures and get the total correct in nine cases out of ten on the first try. But it took me many hours to do it. Nowadays, few young men can add ten figures with any assurance of being correct the first time; but anyone can learn to manipulate an adding machine which will give the correct total of many millions of figures in a few moments' time. Sixty years ago it took my father and me a night and a full day to go from New York City to Troy, New York, a little above Albany, by boat and train—even more, for the train broke down. But nowadays one can fly to Troy and beyond in less than an hour's time.

These are simple illustrations of the change which has

come about within a generation or two as a result of the vast strides in mechanical invention. We have not only eliminated time and space, but leisure and peace, thought and contemplation; and our streamlined life is supposed to fill the vacuum. The massing of capital has given us the noise and speed which fill all our waking hours. Habits of leisurely studying and thinking seem all but obsolete for the younger generation. I was recently asked by one young woman, "How can anyone in these thrilling days of up-to-dateness spend time on such boresome things as serious study? All our leisure moments are filled to overflowing with the radio, the movies, reading the best sellers, or motoring and airplane flying. Isn't that 'education' enough?"

We elderly people who have lived through this evolution in ways of living, often find it hard to adjust ourselves to it all. But it would seem that the rising generation love to live at this high tension, certainly so in our highly mechanized city life. Every motion is a wasted motion unless pitched at rapid tempo. There are no slow coaches any more; only high-speed motors. When a boy, to drive a horse twenty miles a day was for me an achievement; but now to drive an automobile five hundred miles a day is no achievement at all.

That is the sort of life enrichment that has descended on our modern world—for those who can afford to indulge it—for those who have the wherewithal and do not have to struggle for their daily bread. Not so, however, for the masses. As for the latter—it might be well to sketch this modern life enrichment as we find it functioning among the millions of city dwellers of our time; those whose lives are filled with labor. Here is the picture.

The sun is rising on a winter morning; the light of a new

day is beginning to penetrate the homes of several millions of human beings, who must continuously breathe the fetid air of the modern wonder city. The streets and avenues, comparatively quiet an hour before, are resuming their roar of traffic, as the taxis, motor buses and private motor cars begin anew their daily round hither and yon. The tramping of feet on the pavements, the shouts of traffic policemen, the tooting of horns, the screaming of sirens, the blowing of whistles on land and water, all contribute to the pandemonium. The two great gods of modern life, noise and speed, have awakened to another day.

With the dawning of this new day, several millions of men, women and children are stirring in their beds, or hurrying into their clothes, or gulping down their breakfasts. Soon, a million or more children are rushed off to the schools, and millions of adolescents and grown-ups are hurrying to their daily toil. A hundred thousand elevators dash up and down, emptying flats and apartment houses, boarding and lodging houses, hotels, tenements and rookeries, and filling up office buildings, stores and factories. The morning subway rush is on, with scores of thousands of men and women jostled and hustled, jammed and crushed, as the trains pull in and then start up again and tear through the dark tunnels under the city, annihilating time and space to the tune of their own particular roar; while buses, under-river tubes, bridges and ferries are speedily pouring another million or two humans into this great maw of enterprise and industry.

As the day advances, the two great gods, noise and speed, manifest themselves in a thousand other ways. In the offices, stores and factories millions of typewriters, calculating machines and other mechanical devices rattle and bang;

thousands of wheels and gadgets develop their own particular noise in every factory. Department stores and shops fill up with buyers and bargain hunters, who rush hither and thither to the tune of endless chatter, argument and dispute. Housewives jostle one another and fight for place and for bargains at the markets; pedestrians throng the avenues, ladies of leisure flock to the beauty parlors and millinery shops; while all day long and far into the night, cafés, restaurants, night clubs, hotel dining rooms and coffee shops add to the din, if not with canned music and cabarets, at least with the shouts and laughter or quarrelling of more or less boisterous or half-sober guests. And all the while—far into the night with many—several millions of laboring humans are painfully, nervously and in many cases breathlessly at work manipulating machinery, turning wheels or screws, pushing pens or vacuum cleaners—all as cogs in the intricate machinery of large-scale production and distribution, which is the child of this highly mechanized, inventive age in which we live.

It might be assumed that the weary working population of this wonder city, having lived through its day of uproar, tumult and clamor, would crave some degree of peace and quiet for its evening hours. But not so; nerves are too ragged for that. Bigger and better noise is what is sought for. Haggard and exhausted men and women, by the thousands, rush home after the roar and tumult of the day, to consume their evening meal or devote their evening hours, to the tune of oratory, slapstick or mechanized music, by listening in on the radio.

And in a very real sense the great god noise, is matched by the great god, speed. In days long past most people loved to take their recreation with at least a modicum of poise and leisure. But in this modern screaming age, the tall talker, the loud speaker and the fast worker get the center of the stage. The seething population, buffeted through its day of high-speed struggle to survive, now wants not rest but thrills. And it hurries out to get these thrills at the movies; or crowds Town Hall or some other rendezvous to be thrilled by hair-raising proclaimers of streamline wisdom of one sort or another. There are the faddists with their "isms"; the fakirs and promoters of nut religions and philosophies, the spiritualists and the table-rappers, the star gazers, the wise men from the East, and all the other rackets so dear to the hearts of the discouraged and confused—and to the nondescript army of the gullible. Also the parlor pinks and the full blooded reds. And always looming large for many are the night clubs. A strenuous life, if not a happy one, for all.

2.

Such is a brief glimpse of our modern mechanized age of resplendent scientific advance, as it expresses itself in the lives of the vast majority of city dwellers. This is the "civilized level of high degree, such as has never before been known in history."

But, it will be contended by some that this is only the hectic side of our streamlined age. Even for these struggling masses, life is marked with many blessings unheard of in earlier days. We have overcome scores of handicaps of the horse and buggy age. The advance of science has perfected our ways of living as well as of thinking, what with our modern methods of sanitation, with motors for all but the very destitute, with all sorts of specialists in free clinics to supplant the old-fashioned all-round doctor; with progressive education for the young; and also with the "planned" family now possible by the simple methods of birth prevention, the easing of divorce laws, the countryside decline of religious beliefs and consequent easing of personal discipline, and so and so on. If men and women must live faster, they can at least live freer.

Moreover, modern inventions have all but eliminated the weariness of walking; for a mere nickel we can always ride. We need no longer cook; factory pie is fine and every drug store is an eating place. Nor need we spend time reading fact or fiction, trying on a suit of clothes, testing out a motor gasoline or choosing a particular brand of soap; we can get the "low-down" on these and scores of other things by listening in on the radio. In short, we possess a myriad of comforts our ancestors never dreamed of having. Life for all, rich or poor, has been enormously enriched.

Yes, indeed! My grandfather probably never had a bathroom in his house, not to mention bathroom gadgets. He never spoke through a telephone or turned on an electric light. He never had a chance to spend his substance, financial or mental, on things like night clubs; he might visit a theatre once or twice a year, but he couldn't haunt the movies every night. He had no radio; he might get the news once a day but not all day long. If a war broke out in Siam or Sumatra, he might hear of it within a month or two; but if a kinglet was murdered in Somaliland, he would probably never hear of it—thank God!

Still, grandfather did have some advantages that you and I can never have and could do some things you and I can never do. While he could not drive a motor he could ride a horse; while he could not shoot across the Continent in the air, he could shoot a bear or buffalo; while he could not knock a little white ball around a golf course, he could fell a tree and walk a dozen miles after doing it. He had no flashy magazines nor filthy books to read, but he could get a kick out of the classics. He had no labor union to cut down his working day from twelve hours to six or seven, but somehow he had more leisure for the worth-while things of life than I can ever manage to find. And he was never too tired on Saturday night, after a week of toil, to be up and coming and spick and span for going to church on Sunday morning.

We think grandfather lived in benighted times. I am now nearly as old as he was when he died and I live in this wonder age of life's enrichment. Yet how soft I am compared to him. Trying to walk a dozen miles a day would promptly put me in my grave. I can no more ride a horse than I can ride a camel. And if I couldn't motor daily to my office six or seven miles away, I would simply have to retire from business. And although I have few excuses for feeling tired on Saturday night, I find it no easier to be up and coming and spick and span for going to church on Sunday morning.

And so, after all, one wonders, if one is looking for life enrichment—even if one can afford to enjoy its so-called blessings—whether one gets it by living in the streamlined strata of this wonder age. My own life has been blessed in many ways beyond compare; but for the bulk of humanity in our wonder cities, whether liberally blessed with this world's goods, or forced to struggle to keep body and soul together, life would appear to be far more of a tragedy than a blessing. It seems far more difficult in these days of mechanized living than was the case in simpler times, for one to develop character, grow strong and rugged, be just and unselfish, and, withal, "keep one's soul unspotted from the world." And to a marked degree the latter was one of the things grandfather surely did.

Yet perhaps it might be said in passing that grandfather approached the spiritual side of life somewhat differently from the way many of us do nowadays. For instance, it would have been far more difficult for him to have become a Catholic than it was for me. He was a good pious Protestant, and I surely fear he would have thought himself suffering in sin if he had ever accepted the Catholic view that it would be all right for him to read newspapers on Sunday or go fishing on that holy day. He would have felt that his life could not be enriched by adopting this Catholic code of toleration.

But as I have already indicated in these pages (and here parenthetically repeat) it was quite different with me. Living practically all my life in the environment of a wonder city, struggling for a living and for enrichment from my fifteenth year onward, delving into all sorts of theories and fancies for mental and possibly spiritual growth—but being much influenced by the philosophy of materialism just outlined—my journey to the Catholic Church was necessarily an emergence not only from a jungle of contradiction and confusion, but from that state of mind so vividly depicted in the apostle's words—"being without hope and without God in the world." Far more than grandfather, I knew all about "suffering in sin" long before I knew anything about the Catholic Church.

3.

An acute modern scholar was recently asked to give a correct definition of the word "philosophy." And this was his reply: "Philosophy is the attempt, by reasoning, to know the ultimately real." An accurate definition.

I was one day discussing this definition with a thoughtful business man who is himself something of a student of life and a strong endorser of what he calls "modern enlightenment." Being a convinced atheist also, he fully endorsed the conclusions of the aforesaid writer on mass production and distribution as the creator of all happiness that man can hope for in this life; the only life, in his view, that man can ever hope to know. "I readily admit," he said, "that this view gives life a dubious outlook. But that's all there is to life; and that being so, we should seek our happiness by enriching our short lives as far as possible with the goods of this world."

That, to him, was the "ultimately real" of human life. There was a time when I might possibly have agreed with him—at least to a degree—but no longer. He, with the typical atheistic or agnostic mind saw life on the surface only, not in its depths. And I recollect then and there launching a discussion on the subject, primarily from the Catholic standpoint. A little of this is appended.

"Being an atheist, you perhaps never enter churches; certainly not Catholic churches. You are quite sure that Christianity in this country is drying up, anyway. You hear of the despair of preachers to hold their congregations; of the decline and splitting up of sects and the sporadic upshootings of new ones. You note the hosts of people who have wandered away from the religious practices and beliefs of their parents, some seeking solace in non-Christian movements, some relapsing into general unbelief and agnosticism. You perhaps see statements to the effect that more than half the American population have no church affiliations whatever, and that this tendency is increasing. And you deduce from these facts that the old orthodoxy, involving belief in God and in human immortality, is being viewed more and more as an exploded superstition? Am I not right?"

"You are right and you are wrong," he replied. "You are right when you say I believe these facts demonstrate that belief in human immortality is dying out and giving place very fast to more realistic thinking. But you are wrong when you assume that I never enter Christian churches. I often go to church to hear sermons by worthwhile preachers, and again and again I have noticed that nowadays they quite consistently sidestep doctrines and dogmas or blur their meaning. They talk ethics, duties, obligations, the golden rule, and so on. And I do believe in such things, even though I am probably lax in their practice, like all the rest of humanity."

"Yes, I know. You go to churches where Christianity is no longer preached—or only incidentally preached. But you never go into Catholic churches. If you did you might begin to wonder why Catholic Christianity still draws so many people—in view of the crowds you would see. For you wouldn't find any sidestepping of doctrines and dogmas, or blurring of their meaning."

"No, I wouldn't wonder; I would know the answer. It attracts the ignorant and superstitious, no doubt; but I don't believe it attracts intelligent people."

"Thanks for the soft impeachment, old man," said I with a smile. "It attracted me!"

"Oh, well, there are exceptions; you always were an old sentimentalist. You will drop it some day. But you know as well as I, that the masses always lag behind in progress and enlightenment. They never rise to the intelligent level of those who have had the initiative to build this country to its recent condition of progress and prosperity."

"That's the view usually taken by those who know nothing about the 'ultimately real,' " I commented. "If the 'ultimately real' is only attainable by those who have financial affluence in this workaday world, and is measured by temporary comforts and satisfactions, then human life is nothing but a practical joke. Not only a joke on the mass of struggling humanity, who never possess wealth, but spend their lives as cogs in the wheels of this mechanized wonder age; but it is also a joke on you and me. You no doubt possess a plenitude of comforts and luxuries; you never need worry about dollars and cents. But, after all, do you find that these things add anything to your life's enrichment? As far as I have been able to observe, most people who possess the material comforts and satisfactions of this wonder age, are usually restless, dissatisfied and unhappy."

"No doubt," he admitted. "But isn't that because we too readily allow ourselves to reflect on the mutability of human life? As there is no 'ultimately real,' as you style it, outside this earthly existence of ours, all our strivings for comfort, pleasure and happiness are marked by a certain futility; they end when we end. In that sense I agree that human existence is a practical joke. But we must make the best of it; and making the best of it means, in my opinion, improving our ways of living all we can. And we can best do this as a whole by raising the level of our material civilization. That is why I think this book on Capitalism the Creator, proving the importance of mass production and the concentration of capital in the hands of the intelligent minority of inventive master minds, points the true road towards the only life enrichment that we humans can ever hope to know."

"I get you, brother," I remarked as we parted. " 'Eat, drink and be merry, for tomorrow we die!' "

4.

Such conversations are common enough nowadays, even in the marketplace. But most pagans or non-Christians, unlike their ancestors, are not as a rule aggressively antagonistic towards one's religion; not even towards the Catholic religion. They are just aggressively indifferent. They willingly tolerate your religious views, provided you do not try to convert them.

Occasionally, however, you may be confronted by some agnostic or atheist—usually an old one of the vintage of the 1890's—who is not so indifferent; who is bitterly antagonistic towards your religion and goes out of his way to tell you so. And yet it came as a surprise to me last year when an old friend of forty years standing, whom I had not seen for a long time, and whom I had always classed as being tolerant towards those who disagreed with him, turned out to be bitterly intolerant of my Catholicity; as bitterly intolerant as a seventeenth-century Puritan in London.

I had been in the Church nearly nine years when this old friend of far-off days learned of it. At once he wrote me a caustic letter, a shocking letter; for while I had had many a brickbat of this sort hurled at me by strangers, this was the first and only one hurled at me by any old friend. But let me outline the circumstance—and the sequel.

In the days of our youth this friend had been an aggressive champion of revolutionary thought; a protagonist of the coming Utopia in the affairs of men. He had tried to inoculate me with much of this. He was far ahead of me in advocacy of the nihilism of the day. Well do I recall how, as my guide, philosopher and friend, he had persuaded me to read much of Kant and Hegel, of Haeckel and Nietzsche, and finally of Karl Marx (what a headache to struggle through *Das Kapital!*). He had also expounded to me the "meaty" ideas of Tom Paine and Robert G. Ingersoll. Echoing the wisdom of all these masters then seemed the very acme of intellectual erudition. He invariably had answers for every objection, explanations for getting around every difficulty. And in addition to all his other talents, his mastery of words and phrases was superb.

All that, however, was long ago. I had been out of touch with him for years, had half assumed that he was dead. His letter seemed like a voice from the grave. It awoke ancient memories; memories of those days, more than forty years ago, when he so clearly foresaw the impending progress towards the millennium which would surely mark the ensuing years. I naturally wondered how this old-fashioned agnostic would attempt to justify his theories now. And instead of consigning his letter to the waste basket—as I usually do with similar ones from strangers—I replied to him at length. I knew how best to write him—playfully— for I hadn't forgotten how painfully serious and intent he had always been. My reply was more or less frivolous, pouring gentle sarcasm on his old revolutionary creed, and twitting him aimably about the awful state in which we now find the world as a consequence of the gospel he had preached so strenuously forty years before. No doubt irritated at my frivolity, he shortly thereafter came to see me, to "have it out" he said, as he ignored my smiling welcome.

His appearance shocked me. He was now an old man past seventy, in poor health, quite broken, his days obviously numbered. A startling contrast to the upstanding youth of forty years before, then all fire and vim, with flashing eyes and intently serious mien—a true crusader of enlightenment. Now his eyes were dull, his speech halting, his movements deliberate and slow, and his body racked with pain. At once I regretted having written that irritating letter. And yet I could not help but view him as a striking symbol of the breaking down, in our present day, of the modern creed of economic determinism, which we young squirts of forty years before so strenuously tried to preach to a credulous world.

We lunched together that day and talked for hours. He had come all primed to castigate the Catholic Church rather than defend his own agnostic views of life. He started in with hammer and tongs before we had finished the soup. I let him rattle on as he painted the Church jet black with great splashes of distorted history, false statements and general ridicule and abuse—the old, old method of those who bitterly hate the Church and desperately grab at anything within reach to fortify that hate. Once again I heard all about the Scarlet Woman of Babylon, the pathetic case of poor Galileo, the burning of Bruno, the machinations of the Jesuits, the atrocities of Torquemada and of the Spanish Inquisition, the massacre of St. Bartholomew, the fires of Smithfield, the immorality of Alexander VI. But not one word about Catholic doctrine or dogma.

I believe we had reached the pumpkin pie when he had exhausted the supply of rhetoric he had been industriously mixing to make his jet black paint. He paused in triumph. He had worked himself up to such a state that he had begun to sputter at the mouth, and I really didn't see how he could masticate the pie. But I ate mine with relish, offered him a deadly black cigar and then started in with my rebuttal.

"Now that you have painted the Church so black that it is only a messy smudge, let us get down to cases. How is your friend Hitler? And your friend Stalin?"

"Hitler? What have I got to do with Hitler? Stalin isn't so bad, but you can't pin Hitler on me. He's a rascal."

"Your own philosophy, the philosophy you shouted from the housetops when we were boys, pins Hitler on you; and pins Stalin on you too. You, who always bragged of your logical mind, must know that. You are bound to see eye to eye with Hitler and Stalin. If men are mere animals, without immortal souls, as you believe, why is not Hitler doing the right thing, following the right method, for building up the heaven on earth you always foresaw? If the State is everything and human beings nothing but slaves of the State, why not liquidate those who refuse to obey? It's all beautifully logical, starting with the premise that men are merely educated animals."

"Hold on a minute," he interjected; "that's all sentimental rot, emotional stuff you're giving me. You are trying to twist the issue. Liberal thought doesn't stand for Hitler——!"

"But it plays into the hands of Hitler—and Stalin. They are the same thing. Don't you realize, old man, that this cataclysm, which is engulfing the world, is nothing but the outcome of the wide belief of today that God is a mere figment of the imagination; that the grave is our only destiny?"

"Oh, you are wrong. The world is full of fools, I admit

that; most men are stupid, they don't understand the law of human progress. What is needed is education, and more education. The world is ignorant—and in this country it's the fault of the Catholic Church which keeps people ignorant. Let me read you a recent pronouncement of Dr. Dewey and a large group of great thinkers which I clipped from the paper; it is a clear, concise statement of fundamental truth." He drew the clipping from his pocket and read it.

It was a scrap from a so-called religious manifesto issued in 1930 and signed by a group of educators and "humanists." Among these signers were well-known agnostics like Harry Elmer Barnes and John Dewey. It read as follows:

We regard the universe as self-existing and not created. We believe that man is a part of nature and that he has emerged as a continuous process. We reject the traditional dualism of mind and body. We assert that modern science makes unacceptable any supernatural or cosmic guarantees of human values. We consider the complete realization of human personality to be the end of man's life.

"There," he exclaimed, "is a scholarly statement of truth. It is signed by great modern thinkers, including seven thoughtful Christian ministers. That's the sort of Christianity I understand."

"You mean it's the kind you and Hitler and Stalin understand," I commented.

"You are just plumb crazy. Bringing in Hitler and Stalin is pulling a red herring across the trail. I tell you the day will surely come when men will be men. The rise of mankind will go relentlessly on. It is going on now. Think of the strides from the creeping oxcarts of the primitives to the high-powered automobile of today."

"Yes, and think of the mechanized armies, the air bombers and submarines which are destroying mankind today—all products of your great scientific advance; all the outcome of your philosophy."

We talked on in this strain all the afternoon. But it was no good. I wish I could say that the old dreamer was impressed, but obviously he was not. And recently he died; borne down by ill health and years, he was gathered to his fathers just as the Nazis marched into Paris. Happily he did not hear of that; he had worshipped the French; Voltaire and Rousseau had always been his great pioneers of the enlightenment. No doubt honest and sincere, but saturated with the teachings of those who laid the foundations of our present era of hate and despotism, he ended as an unhappy victim of this materialistic philosophy which teaches that the only life enrichment man can ever know is his degree of success in achieving worldly comforts and satisfactions.

5.

I had no intention of crowding this chapter with the views of atheists and agnostics, but it has seemed necessary to do so in order to indicate what is *not* life's true enrichment. I trust I have succeeded to at least a slight extent.

Perhaps many of us have noticed that numerous modern business and professional men who have lived through their careers without giving much thought to the things of the spirit, struggling mightily and often feverishly for material advancement as the only "ultimately real," are prone to stop and wonder in their last sobering years if, after all, the game they played was ever worth the candle. For in nine cases out of ten, when they come to draw up their final balance sheet at the end of life, they find themselves deeply "in the red." For fifty years I have watched them; and if I here jotted down the names of all the suicides in the business and professional worlds I have personally known, the list would more than crowd this page.

We all know that modern streamlined life in business and the professions has a profound effect on character; it tends to make us self-centered, acquisitive and hard-boiled. And perhaps, with a record of over fifty years of business life behind me, it may be suspected that I must have been, to a substantial degree, touched by that hard-headed or hard-boiled quality which tends to induce one to fight shy of subjective sentimentality of every kind. Indeed, I have been. So much so, in fact, that objective reality has long seemed the only thing worth giving much time or thought to. And if I had not found Catholicism outstandingly an objective reality—the fountainhead, not of sentimentalism, but of the "ultimately real"—it would never have interested me.

I say this after having been ten years in the Church. But it didn't take me ten years to decide that Catholicism has the true answer to life; the answer which so many are groping for in this war-torn, tragic era in which we are now living. I discovered this answer in more peaceful times. Catholicism would still be the answer even if we were living in an earthly paradise of peace and justice, and if good will prevailed throughout the world. The ultimate answer to the what, why and wherefore of human existence would be just as insistently needed under such conditions as it is needed now; for no mere earthly paradise could, of itself alone, bring the joy of knowing with certitude that the human spirit is immortal.

No doubt many men—particularly the hard-boiled variety—will laugh if you tell them that Catholicism is "the only answer to life." They will surely brush it aside as a sentimentalism, or perhaps decide that old age is beginning to soften your hard-boiled head. A behind-the-door whisper reached my ears recently which will indicate what I mean. I had told a certain business man during a casual conversation, that Catholicism is, after all, the only answer. And "behind the door" he asked another man what I meant by saying such an extraordinary thing, when all he really wanted to find out was what I thought would become of us if Hitler succeeded in crushing the "democracies." This was the answer he got: "Oh, you mustn't take the old man too seriously since he has gone nutty on religion."

Of course I understand that point of view. I once had it myself. It is not usually based on antagonism to religion. Most men are really religious at heart, even though they may profess no particular faith. Even agnostics have their spiritual fancies. The point of view expressed behind the door is rather due to ignorance of Catholicism nurtured since childhood through false teaching, a prejudiced environment and so on. And often perhaps it is due to the failure of the churches to agree on what is true or not true; a state of things very potent in inducing indifference with many. As Father Ronald Knox said in his *Beliefs of Catholics*, men shrug their shoulders and say, "First let the Churches make up their minds what to believe, and then come and tell me." Such men stand waiting for an answer; but all they usually get is a babel of voices giving them confusing and contradictory answers. And no doubt they assume that it would be the same with Catholicism.

Now I have been too long in the Church to hope that many of my contemporaries will be induced to do what I did; I got over that fond fancy long ago. But well do I know that in these troubled days, with the entire economic and social structure of civilization crashing; with half the world in a vortex of human slaughter; and with the great inventions of modern scientific society being used to wipe out the very civilization they were invented to improve— all sorts of people are bitterly disillusioned with the doctrine of materialistic advance, as the only answer to life.

And so perhaps I do cherish the hope that a few of my contemporaries may be persuaded—or "all but persuaded" —as was King Agrippa by St. Paul, to at least cast their eyes in the direction where the true answer to their confusion lies. When Paul stood before Agrippa, the latter, after listening to his story, exclaimed, "Thou all but persuadest me to become a Christian." And St. Paul replied, "I would that not only thou, but all men who hear me this day would become as I am—save these bonds."

Agrippa was "all but" though not completely persuaded. But at least he listened with attention, apparently, and displayed receptive interest. And that is what, it seems to me, the unsettled and disillusioned men of today should do if they seek peace—at least stop, look and listen at the crossing of the road which leads to life's true enrichment.

*   *   *

In the summer of 1941 a business acquaintance came into my office one morning with a long-faced, haggard look, and finding me smiling and serene, exclaimed:

"How in blazes can you keep smiling in these hellish times? Don't you know that Europe is being destroyed and America soon will be? Don't you know that business is shot to pieces, and that taxes are mounting to the moon?"

"Why shouldn't I be smiling?" I quietly replied. "You see, old man, I went to early Mass this morning."

That's where one finds true life enrichment. But, not being a Catholic, he didn't understand.

Chapter Twelve

WHAT, WHY, WHEREFORE?

I.

"NOT BEING a Catholic, he didn't understand." Thus the last line of the last chapter. No, he didn't understand—even though he reacted to my words with a quiet nod and an awesome glance.

There is a line in Emerson's essay on "Self Reliance" which runs as follows: "To be great is to be misunderstood." Emerson's contention was that all the great teachers of mankind have been invariably misunderstood by the multitude. True enough; but the fact is even more universal than that; it applies to everybody. We are all of us being misunderstood by one another all the time. I recall that as a boy I used to find much satisfaction in quoting that phrase when worsted in an argument, or when realizing that I could not express myself clearly. Often I found it an easy "out" to exclaim: "You don't understand; but after all, as Emerson said, 'To be great is to be misunderstood.'"

That was a boyish satisfaction when worsted in an argument; a sort of coddling to my vanity. It never really got me anywhere. Yet I never forgot those words, and through the years they often consoled me when nettled by someone who contradicted me. Even now they come to my mind when I hear the absurd notions of the Catholic Faith held by some people. And they come to my mind also at this hour, as I glance over the pages of this book and wonder if all will clearly grasp the meaning of many references to the Catholic Faith which dot its pages. Still, I do not find any "greatness" in this circumstance. It is surely great to be a Catholic, despite the fact that your Catholicity is not understood. But there is little satisfaction in realizing that some people persist in utterly misunderstanding or misinterpreting it, regardless of all your efforts to explain it to them.

The late Monsignor Joseph H. McMahon of Our Lady of Lourdes Church, New York City, said to me shortly before he died:

"I have spent my long life trying, in my feeble way, to enlighten many non-Catholics on the simple fundamentals of the Catholic Faith—the 'what, why and wherefore' of the Church. But to a large degree it has been a hopeless task. While there has been a noticeable decline in anti-Catholic bigotry and prejudice in this country in recent years, clear understanding of even the simple fundamentals of the Faith has not made much advance. Many, a great many, view us kindly, tolerantly; but they don't understand. They simply cannot, or will not, understand."

If the lifelong Catholic is conscious of this attitude on the part of much of the non-Catholic public, the convert is even more conscious of it—in view of his non-Catholic contacts and background. For a full decade as a Catholic I have lived in a general environment which is mainly non-Catholic, and have daily mixed with many who, while tolerant enough towards my religion, seem determined to misunderstand it; determined not to try to understand it. And I have often been puzzled; not at their lack of interest, but because so many of them assume that any sort of religious absurdity is right down my alley. Anything labeled "religion," which is puzzling to them, they assume is somehow "Catholic."

Let me give an example. A few years ago a book appeared called *The Return to Religion*, written by a well-known psychologist; it was a best seller. Within a few months after it appeared, several friends had mentioned it to me as another story of the prodigal son, who, like myself, had "returned to religion." Whether they had read it or not, they assumed that it was a duplicate of my own story. It was a good book and contained some truth; but it certainly would never help anyone to understand Catholicism—but rather to misunderstand it.

I have had, in ten years' time, many similar experiences. People have sent me or recommended books on Buddhism, Rosicrucianism, Theosophy, Vedantaism, Deism and outpourings of other cults, assuming that they were all somehow "Christian," and would therefore interest me. One friend quite innocently recommended Renan's *Life of Jesus* as a defence of Catholic Christianity! Another, Emile Zola's *Lourdes;* and Anatole France's *Joan of Arc* was once pointed out to me as a Catholic masterpiece. But perhaps the most comical incident of my experience was the recommendation to me of Bertrand Russell's *Marriage and Morals* as good Christian literature. Of course, none of these people had ever read any of these books; they judged them by the headlines or by reviews; just as people so often judge the Catholic Church and the news of the day by the headlines —never taking the trouble to find out what is really true.

Having experienced, in the course of years, so many incidents of this sort, I was at one time inspired to write out a brief explanation of Catholic fundamentals for some of these well-meaning but woefully misunderstanding friends. A number of copies were handed to several whom I thought might be interested. Every recipient thanked me heartily, and said he was most eager to learn all about the Catholic Faith. But after a while I discovered that only one of them had bothered to read any substantial part of what I had so laboriously prepared for their enlightenment. They were not sufficiently interested to take any trouble to understand. The truth of Monsignor McMahon's words was amply confirmed. And I thought of the old couplet:

> The search for Truth is not near so pleasant
> As sticking to the views we hold at present.

One thought, back of my mind when writing this book, was to slip into the narrative wisps of Catholic truth whenever the opportunity offered, hoping that by so doing I might help understanding of the what, why and wherefore of Catholic life and doctrine. This I have tried to do to a modest extent. But it is also important to know what the Faith is *not*, as well as to know what it is. An approach to Catholicism by way of elimination surely has its value; especially in these days of confused thought in high places. As some shrewd observer has remarked, many people believe in all there is to the Catholic Church except her doctrines and dogmas. And so, in the light of all this confusion, it may be well to submit a few samples of what Catholicism is *not;* and then follow this with a couple of samples of Catholic fundamentals, which may help to indicate what Catholicism *is*.

Let me assure the reader, however, that he is not now to be afflicted with samples of dry-as-dust theology. I shall

continue to talk in "words of one syllable," as I have been
doing all through. As a matter of fact, the Catholic Faith,
with all its doctrines and discipline, is not an abstruse or
complicated conglomeration of discordant elements, as so
many outsiders assume. It is really as simple as ABC. Quite
obviously it can never be grasped by certain modern philosophers and scientists, whose towering mentalities function without the help of Almighty God, but it can be easily
understood by you and me, and by all of us who are conscious of our mental limitations.

I shall begin by briefly indicating, through the presentation of a few samples, what the Catholic Faith is *not*.

2.

The Catholic Faith is not what many people nowadays
call "liberal" Christianity. What *is* "liberal" Christianity?
An excellent example of it is the confession of faith of a
scholarly person which was recently put into my hands. It
is well worth quoting at some length, if only to show how
far from traditional Christian teaching many modern minds
have wandered. Below are the salient points (in his own
words) of this "liberal" Christian's creed.

"My faith is a wobbly, jittery affair. (1) God, creator,
'father' (though sometimes his fatherhood seems obscured);
imperfectly known, revealed in nature and in personality;
possibly too great to care for individuals (though I try not
to believe that); concerned only with the future of the
race.

"(2) Jesus—the Great Teacher and Master Personality
along with others—now obscured by tradition, legend,
myth—but yet the leading spirit for permanent realities in

civilization—who *saves* those who live his principles (because one is 'lost' who is out of harmony with correct principles of living), who died to prove the reality of spiritual principles, and to give his message the magnetism only sacrifice ever gives.

"(3) Immortality—as a reasonable outcome of personality based on faith in an intelligent created universe.

"(4) Life—with certain spiritual values central.

"(5) Prayer—as man's part in a coöperative creative task —not much 'give' me—as that is mostly arranged anyway —mostly 'harmonize' me with the Great Forces of the universe—only at my disposal when I am in tune for it.

"(6) Man himself—a growing, unfolding character, free to develop or not as he chooses."

Such is this "liberal" Christian's creed. But he added at the end of this confession: "This is not an argument—nor in any sense a suggestion that any of it is permanent or valuable. . . . And, I may add, I envy you any peace or spiritual poise your own view of Christianity creates."

Now that is all sincerely and modestly stated. He is a man of good will; a perplexed seeker of truth. But as he himself states, his faith is a wobbly, jittery affair. It is a signal example of the mixture of truth and error which burdens many honest people who have been taught to rely on their own private judgment for an understanding of Christianity, giving no attention whatever to the plain teaching of Christ and His Church. "He has the parts within his hand, but not, alack, the spirit band." And the "spirit band," of course, is nothing less than belief in the Divine Incarnation—which obviously this man does not recognize at all. That is why his faith is "wobbly and jittery." It is characteristic of all people who rely (as this man does) on their own power to pick and choose; who assume that truth is always to be reached through their own inward consciousness, and that objective evidence is of no importance; who have lost all conception of the supernatural, and ignore divine revelation entirely.

Here is another sample of what the Catholic Faith is *not*. Shortly after I became a Catholic a certain eloquent and very "liberal" type of preacher, whom I had come to know intimately, said to me, "Now that you have skeedaddled over to St. Peter, I will frankly say to you that I am at heart as good a Catholic as you are. Often, before preaching in my own church on Sunday morning, I have slipped quietly into the Catholic church up the street, to spend a little time there in prayer and meditation."

"Why do you do that?" I asked. "You have always told me that every Catholic church is a hotbed of ignorance and superstition."

"So they are," he replied. "But there is an atmosphere of sanctity in a Catholic church which is never found in my own church. I would find it very easy to be a Catholic if I did not have to believe what they teach. The old ritual fascinates me; the Latin Mass is a beautiful drama."

That man may have had a slight nostalgia for Catholicism, but he was very far from it. He freely admitted that he did not believe in the Incarnation! And there are many others like him; they would like to become Catholics if they could do so without believing the Catholic Faith. Which reminds me of a little conversation I once overheard in St. Patrick's Cathedral, New York City, at an early Mass on an Easter morning. A man and woman (evidently husband and wife) in the pew behind me were whispering audibly while Holy Communion was being